# Creativity
## and the
# Standards

**Authors**
John Dacey, Ph.D.
Wendy Conklin, M.A.

SHELL EDUCATION

## Publishing Credits

Dona Herweck Rice, *Editor-in-Chief*; Robin Erickson, *Production Director*;
Lee Aucoin, *Creative Director*; Timothy J. Bradley, *Illustration Manager*;
Sara Johnson, M.S.Ed., *Senior Editor*; Leah Quillian, *Assistant Editor*;
Grace Alba, *Designer*; Corinne Burton, M.A.Ed., *Publisher*

### Image Credits

p.58, LOC [LC-USZ62-44892 ]; p. 78, Getty Images; p. 93, LOC [LC-USZC4-11540];
Photo of John Dacey courtesy of Jim Fesler

### Standards

© 2004 Mid-continent Research for Education and Learning (McREL)

---

## Shell Education

5301 Oceanus Drive
Huntington Beach, CA  92649-1030
http://www.shelleducation.com
### ISBN 978-1-4258-0996-6
© 2013 Shell Educational Publishing, Inc.

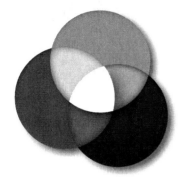

# Creativity and the Standards

## Table of Contents

# Foreword

For far too long, our school systems have been focused on turning out students who are comfortable with conformity—cogs in the machine, capable of following precise directions, and filled to the brim with memorized facts. The problem is that the world has changed forever and those skills and traits are no longer what our kids need to learn to be successful. In fact, the world is changing so rapidly that it's virtually impossible to predict with any certainty what it will look like by the time they graduate. The modern reality requires that successful individuals be able to adapt to change, apply information in new and innovative ways, and work collaboratively to solve problems. Accessing knowledge is no longer the barrier and gatekeeper to learning that it used to be. Today's students can access all of the factual information in the world with a few touches on a device small enough to fit in their pockets. The new key to the kingdom of learning that will allow students to open, unravel, and successfully navigate this increasingly complex world can be summed up in one word...*creativity*.

The challenge is that very few subjects are as shrouded in mystery as creativity. Furthermore, what most people think they know about it is often inaccurate and filled with misinformation. *Creativity and the Standards* not only demystifies the creative process but also offers a clear answer to the two most important questions on the minds of teachers:

1. Can creativity be taught?

2. How can I teach creativity without losing time and focus on the standards?

John Dacey and Wendy Conklin offer a powerfully compelling argument that not only can creativity be taught, but it can be systematically developed and improved upon. Furthermore, utilizing their techniques and strategies will allow students to not only become more creative, but also improve and deepen their understanding of the content standards. In addition, incorporating these creative elements into lessons creates a classroom atmosphere that is absolutely more fun and enjoyable for both students and teachers. It's the ultimate win-win situation!

As a professional development speaker, I can't express how often teachers approach me after my presentations and say they would love to embrace my creative and engaging techniques, but they're worried about how to do so while navigating the high-stakes testing, standards-based world in which we live. *Creativity and the Standards* provides examples after example of just how this is possible. The book is full of standards-based activities from a variety of subject areas and grade levels, and many include examples of student work. There is a real focus on making sure that teachers will be able to immediately and successfully implement the ideas and begin to see the results.

Although I'm an avid student of creativity and frequently speak on the topic, I was pleasantly surprised to find many new strategies and techniques, stopping to write down ideas from every single chapter. I have a whole new set of ideas to add to my teaching toolbox and my students will soon be the beneficiaries. I was particularly taken with the ideas in Chapter Seven: Ten Traits of Creative Students. The advice on how to develop open-ended assignments to allow some autonomy and encourage independent and creative thinking was excellent. The focus on the importance of humor and playfulness in the classroom also deeply resonated with me. The examples of problem-based learning projects that could actually be implemented in the real world were brilliant. My mind is still on fire with the possibilities!

My favorite story from the book is about the young man who is asked how to measure the height of a building using a barometer. That student would be a welcome addition to my class, but I fear too many teachers wouldn't greet his "creativity" with the same enthusiasm. I can't wait for you to read it!

The importance of teaching creativity simply can't be overstated. It's crucial. And yet we also have to live in a world filled with standardized tests and the enormous pressure of preparing students to perform well on them. As a teacher and speaker who has a foot firmly planted in both worlds, I can honestly say that *Creativity and the Standards* offers the perfect solution. This no longer has to be an either/or proposition; teaching creativity and standards can go hand in hand, one enhancing the other. John Dacey and Wendy Conklin have written a book I've been waiting for a very long time.

— Dave Burgess
teacher and professional development specialist

# *Acknowledgments*

Any book with the broad scope of this one has many mothers and fathers. We relied on the detailed advice and trials of our materials from fifteen educational professionals:

Carolina Caldini (teacher)

Dan Miley (teacher)

Dana Steiner (teacher)

John Cawthorne (associate dean, Lynch School of Education, Boston College)

Janet Farnsworth (teacher)

Janice Greer (teacher)

Kathy Vandiver (professor of biology curriculum)

Lee Miller (teacher)

Louise Lipsitz (principal)

Lynne Stinson (principal)

Dr. Maggie Mack (curriculum supervisor)

Maureen Devlin (teacher)

Maureen McKenna (teacher)

Nancy Alloway (teacher)

Nancy Wilson (teacher)

We are extremely grateful to them for their enthusiastic advice. Mrs. Alloway must be singled out with special gratitude for all the hours she allowed John Dacey to spend in her classroom and all the questions she so gracefully answered.

Also, we had the service of four senior college education majors in the Lynch School of Education at Boston College. They served multiple roles as researchers and as materials testers at their student teacher placements. Their work was paid for by a work-study grant under the aegis of John Cawthorne (who, sadly, did not live to see the fruits of his labors with us), and we can't thank them enough for all the time they worked beyond what they were paid for. The students are: Brandy Norton, Amy Caldwell, Hannah Alley, and Jill MacNeil.

We are most grateful for the wonderful team at Shell Education and Teacher Created Materials who helped us so much: Rachelle Cracchiolo, Corinne Burton, Dona Rice, Sara Johnson, and Leah Quillian. All of them have been a joy to work with.

Finally, we want to thank three people without whose help we never could have finished this book: Lisa Doucette, who served tirelessly as research coordinator and resourceful critic of our concepts and strategies, and our dear spouses, Dr. Linda Dacey and Blane Conklin.

# Chapter 1

# What Educators Need to Know about Creativity

## Creative Warm-Up

Look at the drawing and imagine the story behind it. Let your imagination flow freely with little concern for "getting it right." Surprise yourself!

In an age when assessing knowledge of facts has never been easier, many countries are emphasizing and testing students for factual knowledge. Today, problems have never been more complex (e.g., the worldwide economic meltdown), and many countries no longer teach skills that strengthen creative problem solving. Teachers know that creative thinking is important, but there are so many standards to cover and so little time to do it. Somewhere along the line, we as teachers have bought into the belief that standards and creativity cannot coexist. The foundation of this book is to challenge that belief. First, we should discuss what educators need to know about creativity, and then we should look at ways to foster creativity in the classroom while also teaching standards-based lessons.

Think back to the creative warm-up. Did you come up with a story that you feel good about? Do you think your idea for a story would be different from one your next-door neighbor would create? Or did you base your answer on what you felt we expected from you? If you think your story is creative, what makes it creative? What is creativity? Can creativity ever be defined? We think it can. Creativity transcends traditional concepts in order to create transformational ideas that are appropriate for the task at hand.

The student-created poem that follows fits the description of creativity. The student had to creatively introduce an endangered species to his class.

## "Who Am I?

I am white with black **s**pots

I tur**n** color d**e**pending **o**n the seas**o**n

I use sounds and scra**p**e **a**gainst the di**r**t to communicate

I am also kno**w**n as the *Panthera uncia*

**D**o you know who I am?"

*(Hint: Use the gray and bold letters to find out the species.)*

Consider the following assignment in which students produced something creative based on research they completed. An eighth grade student researched the abolitionist John Brown and wrote a thirty-one page book, *Diary of a Strong Abolitionist*, borrowing the style from Jeff Kinney's *Diary of a Wimpy Kid*. Figure 1.1 is an excerpt from the student's book.

**Figure 1.1** Student Sample Excerpt

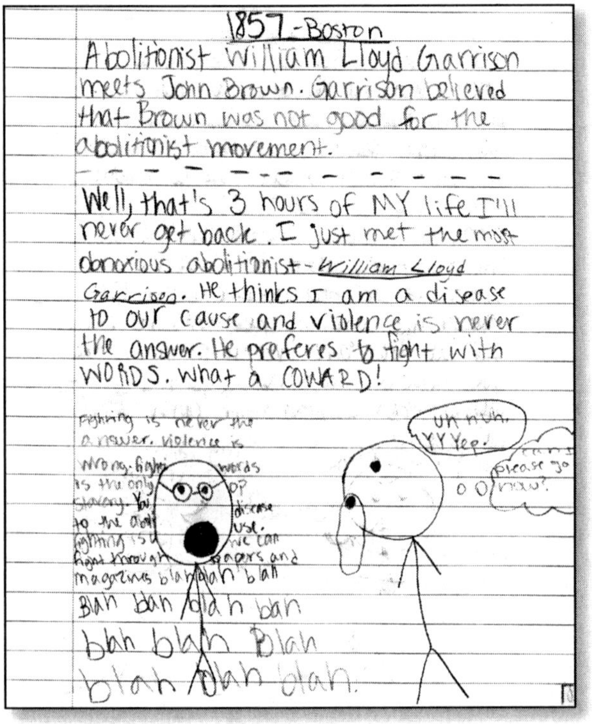
1857-Boston
Abolitionist William Lloyd Garrison meets John Brown. Garrison believed that Brown was not good for the abolitionist movement.
Well, that's 3 hours of MY life I'll never get back. I just met the most obnoxious abolitionist - William Lloyd Garrison. He thinks I am a disease to our cause and violence is never the answer. He preferes to fight with WORDS. what a COWARD!
Fighting is never the answer. violence is wrong.
magazines blah blah blah
Blah blah blah blah
blah blah Blah
blah blah blah.
uh huh. YYYep.
please go now?

Notice the voice and anachronism the student uses to describe how John Brown felt about William Lloyd Garrison. The facts are true—Garrison actually said this about Brown. However, the inclusion of this fact is a product of the student's research. And the student found a way to creatively express it in today's language. What makes students generate creative products like these? More importantly, how can teachers spark creativity in all their students?

The International Center for Studies in Creativity at the University of Buffalo describes the need for students to be able to think creatively. The article states, "There were less than ten technical and social inventions between A.D. 1 and A.D. 1800. Contrast that to the last 210 years, during which time we have seen the creation of more than 25 life-altering technological and social inventions. Inventions that have enhanced the nature and quality of our lives, such as computers, antibiotics, airplanes, the Internet, genetic engineering, organ transplants, automobiles, lasers, telecommunication, etc." (2012, 1).

Around the globe, societies approach the education of students differently. Lately, some societies have been leaning toward teaching content and then evaluating knowledge by using standardized tests, both important pieces of the puzzle in education. Other societies where teaching content has been prominent now seek to strike a more equal balance to include the teaching of creative thinking. The question on many educators' minds is, how do we do both?

## Everyone Has Creative Potential

Creativity is needed by *everyone*. Everyone can learn to be more creative, and there is always room for improvement. The prevalent thought today is that some people are creative and others are not, as if a selected few are given the magical gift. Those of us who don't possess this gift must be content to carry on with the mundane life ordained for us. This type of thinking is wrong. Creativity is something that everyone can achieve, albeit at different levels. It is like a muscle—the more it is exercised, the stronger it becomes (Conklin 2011).

In this book, we will reference creativity in two ways—*extraordinary* creativity and *ordinary* creativity. Extraordinary creativity is the kind we attribute to Einstein, the Beatles, and Picasso. What these individuals produced was life changing. Ordinary creativity is typically the kind of creativity that we can see in our students and ourselves. Creativity is measured on a spectrum. That is, input is presented to the prisms of your students' minds, and a spectrum of creative thinking emerges (see Figure 1.2). Wherever your students are on that creativity spectrum, we will help you lead each of them to a higher level.

**Figure 1.2** Creativity Spectrum

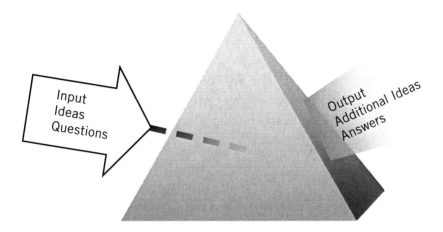

On this subject, the "Full Spectrum"—a term coined by TED (Technology, Entertainment, Design)—of creativity was the theme at the annual TED 2012 Conference in Long Beach, California. Full Spectrum, according to TED, "is a term we've adapted to mean the rich use of multiple technologies, formats, and approaches for the most powerful impact on an audience" and inherently includes the discussion of creativity as many of the TED presentations focused on the creative process. There is likely no place on Earth where creativity is so prized. From 2006 to 2012, more than 1,000 TED presentations have been compiled into one video book (TED 2012). As a source of imagination for smart teachers, you can't beat this resource.

Whether we are children or adults, we are all capable of becoming more creative. And who knows? If we are lucky, we might even witness extraordinary creativity in some of our students.

# What Is Creativity?

Creativity is work. Michael Michalko defines creativity as the "consequence of your intention to be creative and your determination to learn and use creative-thinking strategies" (2006, xvii). It is largely the product of hard work on behalf of the creator. It involves applying oneself in order to produce something—whether that be Michelangelo exploring different techniques using his paintbrush or a student sketching an imaginary plant that could survive in a specific habitat.

Creativity requires perseverance and grit (Lehrer 2012). Creative people still have to work hard to achieve products. Ideas don't just mysteriously float around in the sky and latch onto a person. Often, a person struggles with a problem for a while before finding the right answer. Failure is not a bad thing, and it plays an important role in creativity. Legend has it that Thomas Edison said that he did not fail 2,000 times when trying to create electric light. Instead, he learned 2,000 ways not to make it. It's these perceived "failures" that lead us to success (the 2,001st time!). After a fire destroyed his laboratory, Edison said, "There is great value in disaster. All our mistakes are burned up. Thank God we can start anew" (quoted in Clemmer 2012, 16).

A person may be focusing on ideas or writing sentences that get deleted over and over. But when the right answer is found, the person knows it immediately. The solution is clear. This experience is the same for our students. In societies where acquiring knowledge is immediate through the use of various forms of media, students must be given opportunities to struggle. They can be presented with unanswerable questions, open-ended questions, and opportunities to brainstorm. Students also need a safe place to fail, and this does not mean failing grades. It means failing at finding the answers right away or having an experiment not work out the way it was intended it to. Failure in this sense means learning to tackle difficult tasks and keeping at it, not knowing what the final answer might be. If students never grapple with difficult tasks, they will not learn perseverance and grit.

Creativity demands rigorous thinking within the context of play and fun. The fact that people can enjoy rigorous work is what makes the work tolerable and attractive. There is a huge payday at the end—whether the payoff is the production of something creative or the benefits that come from practicing creativity—creativity makes a person more expressive and confident. Educators should not shy away from planning creative activities. Learning should be enjoyable. Rigorous thinking in creative contexts is productive for our students because it pushes them to search for potential solutions in an engaging manner. For example, a lesson about characterization may ask students to select their favorite character from a television show. One student may select a character from a popular cartoon, another student may select a character from a sitcom, and a third student may select a character from a mystery series. Each student should list the top three attributes of his or her character. Next, in groups of three, students should bring their lists together and combine them to create a brand new character. In the process, they should create, evaluate, and wrestle with how to do this. Rigorous? Yes. Fun? Definitely. This type of creativity is hard work within the context of play and it also teaches about characterization and attributes. A teacher could extend this lesson to show how characters affect the setting and plot of a story.

Creativity includes both divergent and convergent thinking. Divergent thinking is the ability to think of many different ideas fluently. Brainstorming is a perfect example of divergent thinking; all ideas are collected, written down, or thought of. Convergent thinking is the evaluation of ideas' worth by sifting through the ideas to find the best one. Creative individuals use both divergent and convergent thinking as they create, cycling through both thought processes as many times as necessary.

Teachers can encourage creative thinking by using certain strategies, some of which we explain in this book. As with any teaching strategy, the idea is to use the creative-thinking strategy with relevant standards-based content because we know that basing strong lessons on these standards is key to ensure that students learn what they should in each class.

In the past, some teachers have used creative-thinking strategies as fun assignments that students do after the "real work" (i.e., lessons based on standards) is completed. Typically, only the brightest students finish their work early, so they are the only ones who have opportunities to stretch their creative thinking. But it doesn't have to be this way. Creative thinking strategies are like any other good teaching strategy in that they can be used with important standards-based content. Depending on the content, some strategies will be a better fit than others. While the brainstorming strategy might work well with *any* content that has opportunity for brainstorming ideas, the Creative Problem Solving (CPS) strategy might only work with *some* content where there are opportunities for problem solving. It will be up to the teacher to decide which strategies fit best. This content will be based on important standards that must be covered.

The steps to making this work efficiently and effectively should begin by becoming familiar with the creative-thinking strategies outlined in this book. Then, consider the standards-based content that needs to be taught for your students. Finally, put the two together and look for creative-thinking strategies that can complement the outcomes of the lesson. Students will benefit from not only learning important standards-based content but also from the opportunity to enhance their creativity.

## The Teacher's Role in Creative Thinking

There are several things teachers can do to encourage creative thinking in the classroom. First, teach students about those who are *extraordinarily* creative. To begin, explain that in terms of creativity, extraordinary individuals are those who deviate from the norm—they break the rules for a creative end. The Beatles fit this model of extraordinary creativity. Diagramming songs shows that music typically follows a predictable structural pattern: introduction, verse, chorus, another verse, and then a chorus repeated a few times. There might be a bridge before the final chorus is repeated. These structurally ordinary songs sell, and that's why song producers are not willing to take risks by straying from the typical structure of a song. Encourage students to listen for this pattern in the songs they hear on the radio. Extraordinary individuals like the Beatles, however, deviate from the norm. Have students compare the song structures they hear on the radio to the song structures of a handful of Beatles songs. The Beatles burst onto the music scene of the 1960s as a cultural phenomenon and innovative musicians. If we focus only on their songwriting, we see that they broke all the structural rules. Some of their songs begin with the chorus. Others have a verse, verse, verse, verse until the chorus finally plays. And amazingly, their songs work. And they work well. What they did was original. These extraordinarily creative individuals are models of inspiration for us all. Instead of feeling intimidated, we are in awe of what the human mind is capable of producing. Our students will feel that, too, and will learn to appreciate the talent and courage shown by these creative individuals.

Next, show students that you value creative work. Comment on students' work, pointing out where you see their creativity. Let them know you appreciate it, and encourage more of it in their work. Then, show them how you are being creative, too. Share with them your writing, hobbies, passions, and other creative outlets. Be the inspiration for your students.

Finally, use the strategies in this book to spur creative thinking. Use the examples as models for how to integrate these strategies into standards-based lessons. Think of new ways to include these creative-thinking strategies into lessons you already teach. As we all know, teaching demands creativity from teachers. Good teachers are always thinking, "How can I get students to understand this concept?" It is not too big of a stretch to take teaching to the next level by including these strategies to get students thinking more creatively.

The following chapter lays the foundation for the rest of this book. It outlines three models of creativity, the last of which serves as the structure for this book. The subsequent chapters contain creative teaching strategies to implement in the classroom, in addition to management ideas to ensure your success.

 ## Let's Think and Discuss

1. What does the word *creativity* mean to you?

2. In what ways have you noticed creativity in your students?

3. What do you think your deficits are in regards to teaching creative thinking?

# Models of How Creative Thinking Works

## Creative Warm-Up

Kelly Dacey-Hensor is a kindergarten teacher. She tells this story about her student Brandon's power of observation:

Brandon:    *Miss Dacey, what's that red stuff on your mouth?*

Kelly:    *Why, Brandon, that's called lipstick.*

Brandon:    *Why do you put it on your mouth?*

Kelly:    *Because I think it makes me look pretty.*

Brandon:    *Well, maybe you should put some more on.*

Can you think of a funny story drawn from your own teaching experience or a colleague's? What made it humorous? Was there an unexpected twist? Write down the experience, and then analyze what made it humorous. Whether the experience was intentionally or accidentally humorous, if a story is funny, there was most likely a surprising twist. Every joke writer knows this. How does this relate to the concept of creative thinking?

It would be difficult to find a teacher who has not studied Erikson's eight stages of psychological development (Erikson 1963) in a child psychology course. It would also be rare to find an exceptional teacher who could name more than Erikson's first stage, "basic trust," much less what Erikson's crises that accompany each stage are about. Does this mean this teacher's study was a waste of time? Definitely not.

Those concepts settle in your unconscious mind. The better you learned them, the better established they become. One way we know this is that if you were to study Erikson again, you would relearn the material faster and better. More importantly, you are better prepared to teach students than if you had never studied Erikson. You are probably not an expert on Erikson's theory, but having studied Erikson makes your teaching of a higher quality than a nonprofessional who has never studied child psychology (Boeree 2012).

That's how it may be with the models we will describe. You should seek to grasp them as fully as possible because they will make you a better teacher. In particular, you will be a much better teacher of creative thinking. You may forget some of the specifics, but basic tenets will remain with you in your unconscious mind. The unconscious mind is the mental space that gives birth to so much creative thought.

Additionally, the strategies and activity suggestions are specifically based on the three models you are about to read. For example, Torrance's concept of fluency is exemplified by the strategy of negative brainstorming, which can be used to teach standards that address how specific ideas had an impact on history. When you have a better idea of how it all works, it is almost magical how you begin to think more creatively as an educator. You will also get better at recognizing and cultivating creative thinking in your students. All of this happens unconsciously and deliberately, and you will become a better teacher!

The media are filled with tips about how "*You* can be more *creative!*" Some of these tips do actually work. One tip, for example, is to step away from problems. When you do this, you relax the frontal (logical) lobes of your brain (Slade 2012). Old ideas reassemble during this incubation period or stepping-away time. After an allotted amount of time working creatively on a task, have students take a break and work on a different task. This gives the students' brains time to incubate and unknowingly think about the ideas or problems. When they come back to it, they will have a clearer idea of how to solve the problem.

Another helpful tip is to group creative thinkers who have different specialties. Combine thinkers from different backgrounds and watch the sparks fly. Steve Jobs, the late CEO of Apple®, installed only two large restrooms in the company plant so that everyone would talk with people from a variety of specialties at least once a day. In the classroom, instead of forming the same groups all the time, mix up discussion groups often to ensure more creative discussions and problem solving (Lehrer 2012).

*[handwritten margin note: Students work w/ different partners based on time]*

Finally, numerous studies on the development of creative thinking have concluded that creativity declines with increased schooling (Dacey 1989a). This is not the case for everyone, though. According to the studies, it appears that some people maintain their creative ability, regardless of influences that tend to suppress creativity in most others.

In a typical classroom, a few students are quite high in creative ability and a few are low, but the great majority of students are creatively ordinary. This is true of virtually all human abilities—they are "normally distributed." However, the emphasis on answering questions correctly seems to suppress imagination. By the seventh grade, most students' creative abilities range from low to average, and a much smaller number of students retain their creativity. What causes them to be creatively gifted? Can the students who lost some of their creative ability be taught to recover it? Can all students be creative thinkers with the right instruction? Can instruction in creativity actually improve standardized test scores? As you will see, the answer to all of these questions is *Yes!*

The three models of creative thinking—Jackson and Messick's, Dacey's, and Torrance's—are usually called *theories*. We don't refer to them that way; *theory* connotes somebody's educated guess about a concept. We think these models are much more than theory. They have been studied and reported on for a long time (Dacey and Lennon 1999), and they view creativity from different viewpoints, each model contributing to the overall picture. We organize them into a unified whole that will shape the rest of our book.

Finally, let us remind you that in this book, we are only dealing with *ordinary* creativity (Cropley 2011). *Extraordinary* creativity is so unpredictable and high-level that it defies explanation. As Christine Paintner puts it, "When fully enabled and nurtured, [ordinary creativity] can bring to us individuality, new health, satisfaction, and purpose; and together the means to address many challenges of this new millennium" (2011, 687).

## Jackson and Messick's Model

One of the earliest and still one of the best models of creativity is offered by Jackson and Messick (1965). They concluded that creativity has two aspects: the traits of the person and the traits of the product a person creates. Both of these aspects also have two facets: the intellectual and personality traits of the person, and the properties of the creative product and the standard by which it is judged. Finally, each of these facets has four elements. We know this can be confusing, but it will be clearer as we examine each element. This model does a brilliant job of detailing how creativity really works.

**Figure 2.1** Jackson and Messick's Model

| Traits of the Person | | Traits of the Product | |
|---|---|---|---|
| **Intellectual Traits** | **Personality Traits** | **Product Properties** | **Standards** |
| Tolerance of incongruity | Original | Unusualness | Norms |
| Analysis and intuition | Sensitive | Appropriateness | Context |
| Open-mindedness | Flexible | Transformation | Constraints |
| Reflection and spontaneity | Poetic | Condensation | Summary power |

## Tolerance of Incongruity

Tolerance of incongruity is the first intellectual trait of a creative person. Many situations in life seem strange to us. Tolerant people are better able to accept ideas that differ from their own. As a result, they are capable of combining their existing ideas with those that are new to them. Such thoughts usually produce original concepts, and in some cases, they are highly creative.

Steve Jobs fits this description. He was known as a superb inventor, manager, and pioneer of the personal computer. He saw the commercial potential of mouse-driven graphical machines, which led to the revolution called desktop publishing. How was this "incongruous"? Jobs was the first to see this potential. The link was too strange and too ambiguous for others to notice, but he noticed it. He continued to be a visionary throughout his career, not only at Apple® but also at Pixar® and Disney®.

We know when a product is unusual only because we compare it to standards (or norms) to find that the product is rare. For example, as Jackson and Messick put it, "We generally insist as a first step that a product must be novel before we are willing to call it creative" (1965, 317).

## Analysis and Intuition

Some people are described as logical in their thinking. They are able to recall the steps they took to get to a particular conclusion. This is of great value when your principal asks, "And why do you think that?" Others, no less effective in their thinking, use analysis and intuition. This means that thoughts that are buried in their unconscious minds combine with conscious ideas to form solutions to problems they are working on. Then there are those relatively few individuals who are good at both. Furthermore, these people seem to know when to use one mode of thinking over another. Typically, they switch back and forth, knowing when to analyze the problem carefully and when to make an intuitive leap.

Aung San Suu Kyi of Myanmar fits this description. She received the Nobel Peace Prize for her nonviolent struggle for democracy and human rights. She was kept under strict house arrest by the Myanmar government for 15 of the past 21 years. Recently released, she was elected to her country's parliament. Suu Kyi's fight has been one that deals with one ethical problem after another. These ethical dilemmas call for a logical mind (analysis) and a broad "feel" (intuition) for the international nuances of each dilemma.

Such people may be described as highly sensitive. These individuals seem to have special antennae that allow them to grasp complex circumstances. Can this sensitivity be taught? It is not easy, but at least we can give students the chance to practice analysis and intuition. A number of the standards-based activities we recommend in later chapters are designed to provide this practice.

The product of analytical and intuitive thinking tends to be surprisingly appropriate. Jackson and Messick claim that to "be appropriate a product must fit its context, and must make sense in the light of the demands of the situation and desires of the producer" (1965, 315). In other words, such an outcome meets a need. For instance, many people find that listening to outstanding music causes them to cheer up and relax.

## Open-Mindedness

*is this not similar to tolerance of incongruity?*

Open-mindedness refers to the ability to receive new information without prejudice. Why are creative thinkers almost never dogmatic? The way they were raised is probably a major part of the answer. Most parents teach their children to avoid potentially dangerous situations by making them afraid of the consequences. In some cases, this training can be so severe that the child develops phobias. Some parents of creative children are able to find more positive ways to protect their children and encourage their adventurous spirit. When parents foster courage, the child develops a flexible personality. Persons who are flexible tend to be less rigid, less neurotic, and less anxious than others. They also are less authoritarian.

How can you foster this trait in your classroom? In Chapter Four, we go into this subject in detail. Suffice it to say that making your classroom "psychologically safe"—that is, free from excessive emphasis on success and on criticism for failure—is vital.

In any field of human endeavor, there are constraints—that is, there are rules within the field by which the work must be contained. The world's great artistic and scientific achievements rarely involve breaking rules. Rather, they have somehow caused us to understand the rules in new and imaginative ways. For example, the world's highest-earning female made her money in established areas: television with *The Oprah Winfrey Show*, publishing with *O: The Oprah Magazine*, and her book club. Moreover, Oprah Winfrey's insights as an actress in *The Color Purple* and as an educator through her imaginative schools for girls in poor countries mark her as one of the most innovative people in the world today. As a woman operating in a financial world of men, she has had to be both open-minded and flexible. She has had to know when and how to be pleasant and personable, or hard as diamonds.

## Reflection and Spontaneity

The final cognitive trait involves a combination of two extremes: reflection and spontaneity. The reflective approach is a slow, cautious method of problem solving, whereas spontaneity is an unpredictable, risk-taking leap of faith. This trait refers to the speed of the thought process, as opposed to the level of conscious awareness in analysis and intuition.

The creative act often starts with a spontaneous thought followed by reflection on the implications of the idea. Sometimes, however, the process occurs in reverse as it does for novelist Stephen King. He always starts writing the same way because he finds that reflection usually turns into spontaneity. As he puts it, "I have my vitamin pill and my music, sit in the same seat, and the papers are all arranged in the same places. The cumulative purpose of doing these things the same way every day seems to be a way of saying to my mind, you're going to be dreaming soon" (quoted in Rogak 2009, 6). First, he sets himself up to reflect on where he is in the story, and soon, spontaneous insights begin to flow. King's best-selling novels prove his superiority at both types of thinking.

Jackson and Messick use the term "poetic" in its most generic sense; all great achievements are a kind of poetry. These achievments seem to simultaneously unravel complications and get to the heart of the matter. The product is a "condensation." This means the product includes only essential factors, stripping away extraneous pieces. A sculptor literally does this to a block of marble, but it happens not only in the arts but also in the sciences. Consider Einstein's famous formula, $E = mc^2$, which is his theory of relativity. Amazingly, Einstein subsumed the interactions between all matter in how it turns into energy in a formula with just three variables. Now, *that* is condensing! When a product is a brilliant condensation of elements, a single encounter with the product is never enough. Like a superb glass of wine or gourmet meal, we want to savor it.

## Dacey's Model

Are you the kind of person who welcomes problems? The ordinary person doesn't. Most appear to believe that problems are annoying and should be avoided. The difficulty with this belief is that the head-in-the-sand approach often leads to a worsening of whatever fix we may be in. Creative people seem to enjoy the ambiguity of new and challenging dilemmas (Mann 2008). Don't worry if you are the type of person who doesn't like problems. You can teach yourself to welcome them.

According to Dacey's Model (Dacey and Lennon 1999), creativity involves both divergent and convergent thinking. Divergent thinking is characterized by generating several different ideas about a topic. Then, convergent thinking evaluates those ideas and selects the most appropriate one for the task. Both modes of thinking are essential to the alternating process of creative thinking. For example, the ballpoint pen was invented in 1888 but wasn't sold until the 1940s. The pens leaked or clogged, mostly because they depended on gravity to flow. A variety of inks and balls were tried, but it wasn't until someone thought of using capillary action to feed the ink that people started purchasing ballpoint pens. The inventors had to understand the dilemma—Dacey calls this "problem sensing"—but ultimately a flash of insight was needed to resolve it—problem solving. The latter couldn't have happened without the former.

More explicitly, the process is as follows: First, we sense and explore the parameters of a problem through the use of inventive divergent thinking. Then, we narrow down the possibilities by using logical convergent thinking. Once the problem has been clarified, we again use divergent thinking to generate a number of possible solutions. Finally, we evaluate our envisioned solutions by using convergent thinking to select the best solution. Figure 2.2 illustrates this concept. This applies to specific problems, such as how to reduce greenhouse gases as well as to less-defined problems, such as what to paint on a blank canvas.

**Figure 2.2** Dacey's Model

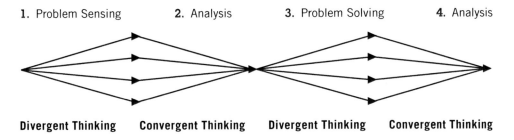

1. Problem Sensing          2. Analysis          3. Problem Solving          4. Analysis

Divergent Thinking     Convergent Thinking     Divergent Thinking     Convergent Thinking

Let's look at Dacey's Model by using an example of extraordinary creativity. Most middle school students know that the sum of the angles in a right triangle is 180° (45° + 45° + 90°). Albert Einstein—an extraordinarily creative individual—knew this, too, but something bothered him about it. He realized that this fact only holds true for two-dimensional space; if you draw a right triangle on a sphere, the answer is different. Suppose you draw a straight line from a spot on the equator to the North Pole at a right angle. Next, you draw another line at a right angle from the North Pole to another spot on the equator. The lines are actually straight, although they appear to bend around the globe. You will see that you have a triangle with three right angles! Therefore, the sum of the angles in this right triangle is not 180° but 270° (90° + 90° + 90°). Figure 2.3 illustrates this concept.

**Figure 2.3** Einstein's Three-Dimensional Right Triangle

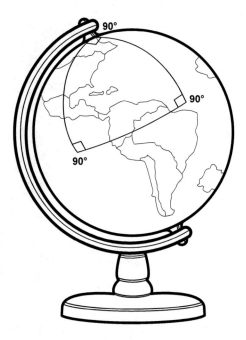

This is the principle that causes plane flights from Europe to America to pass over Greenland. Imagine such a flight superimposed on the globe in Figure 2.3. On this flat picture of the globe, the path appears curved. However, on an actual sphere, such as Earth, you would see that the path is actually straight. Imagine the "ordinary" creativity of the pilot who figured that out!

Einstein soon came to see that all the laws of geometry are limited to two-dimensional space. The universe, however, is three-dimensional. Einstein wasn't the first to realize this, but he stands out because he was one of the first to question and explore this discrepancy, and so began modern-day quantum physics.

We will explain *ordinary* creativity, the kind of creativity that we are all capable of. Through the activities, you will learn how to help your students be sensitive to the problems around them. When a student begins to seek out problems rather than avoid them, intellectual curiosity is born. And as every psychologist knows, a problem that is generated by the individual is much more likely to be carried out than a problem that is provided.

Students who develop this sensitivity to quandaries tend to become eager learners, and thus are much more likely to remember what they have learned. That is why we believe that fostering creativity does not distract from learning in standards-based classrooms. It actually promotes better learning, which results in higher scores on standardized tests, not to mention the value of creative problem solving in today's troubled world.

Figure 2.4 shows a deeper comparison of divergent and convergent thinking, providing a more detailed picture of how Dacey's Model works (based on Helie and Sun 2010). There are seven elements of the process, some of which were drawn from Jackson and Messick's Model. The third column lists reasons why students often give up on finding solutions. Be on the lookout for the six "exits," or escapes, from problems (the seventh is a successful outcome), and try to persuade students not to give up so easily. Perseverance in the face of an obstacle is a major trait of creative people.

**Figure 2.4** Divergent and Convergent Thinking

| Type of Process | Decision-Making Type | Exit from Problem | What a Teacher Might Do |
|---|---|---|---|
| 1. **Preparation**— Explore field prior to creative problem solving | **Convergent thinking**— Identify relevant information leads | **Exit I**— Disinterest | Find more engaging material |
| 2. **Problem sensing** | **Divergent thinking**— Explore that information | **Exit II**—Unable to define worthy problem | Encourage new ways to view the information |
| 3. **Worthy problem identification** | **Convergent thinking**— Choose the problem most worthy of the effort | **Exit III**—Work at a solution is postponed | Discourage procrastination and heighten motivation |
| 4. **Incubation** | **Divergent thinking**— Send problem to the unconscious by switching to another task | **Exit IV**—No useful solution becomes consciously apparent | Teach meditational techniques (see Chapter Eight) |

| Type of Process | Decision-Making Type | Exit from Problem | What a Teacher Might Do |
|---|---|---|---|
| 5. Problem solving | **Divergent thinking**—Be as imaginative as possible to solve the problem | **Exit V**—No "aha" solution appears; further incubation may be necessary | Teach fluency, flexibility, originality, and elaboration methods (Chapters Three through Six) |
| 6. Solution evaluation | **Convergent thinking**—Possible solutions are compared and assessed | **Exit VI**—No solution seems to work | Encourage students to repeat Step 5 |
| 7. Resolution | **Divergent/Convergent thinking**—Back and forth between solutions until satisfied | **Goal achieved**—Success! A suitable solution was chosen! | No work needed. Pat yourself on the back! |

Let's say, for example, that an individual wants to improve the operation of his or her electronics equipment. The picture on the wide-screen TV keeps freezing, and that's irritating. He or she avoids Exit I (Disinterest) because his or her interest in resolving the problem is strong. Then, this individual puts his or her hand into the electronics cabinet and is surprised at how hot it is in there. He or she avoids Exit II (Unable to define worthy problem) because this individual thinks he or she is on to something. This seems like a good lead so the individual decides to think about it some more. After no progress has been made in solving the problem, the decision is made to "sleep on it," avoiding two more exits and allowing for unconscious incubation to occur.

However, in Step 5, it occurs to him or her that the problem may be as simple as poor air flow. The individual then browses the Internet, ultimately finding an article that offers a solution to the problem at hand. He or she evaluates the solution, finds it adequate, and proceeds to create the fan addition, adapting the instructions to fit the needs of the situation. The solution works, and the wide-screen TV no longer freezes. This individual has reached Step 7 without exiting (Goal Achieved—Success! A suitable solution was chosen!).

The fluctuation between convergent and divergent thinking fits well with Jackson and Messick's Model, which also includes constant fluctuation between the thinking styles. The two models do not contradict but complement each other. The third and final model does this, too.

## Torrance's Model

Finally, we come to the model that unifies all we have explained about the creative-thinking process. Ellis Paul Torrance (1915–2003), the godfather of creative problem-solving research, designed the Torrance© Tests of Creative Thinking (TTCT). He based these tests on his seminal four-part model: *fluency*, *flexibility*, *originality*, and *elaboration*. We are not going to explain these four facets in detail here. For the purpose of describing the model, however, we will briefly illustrate how it works through a question we ask in later chapters: "How many uses can you think of for a stone?"

*Fluency* refers to how many ideas the thinker can generate to solve a problem or answer a question. "A stone can build a foundation for a house. It can build a fence. It can build a wall."

*Flexibility* means the number of relevant ideas that are qualitatively different from the other ideas the thinker has imagined. "A stone can build a wall. I can write on a sidewalk with a stone. I can use it as a weapon."

*Originality* refers to the number of relevant answers that are qualitatively different from those produced by the rest of the group thinking about the same problem. "I can use a stone to catch worms. To do this, I can put the stone down on a patch of soil, wait two weeks, and when I pick up the stone, there will be lots of worms on the surface of the soil."

*Elaboration* means the number of ideas produced that clearly enhances the quality of the product in a unique way. "I can tie a rope around the stone, anchor it on a beach at the shoreline, wait a year, and when I recover it, it will be smooth from the action of the waves, revealing a beautiful interior."

Each of these four facets is itself a strategy within the creative-thinking process. Each is also a criterion for assessment. At first glance, these elements may appear to be quite different from those you have read about so far. However, we believe the Torrance Model helps organize all the concepts. Even more useful, Torrance's four criteria of creative thought work well as umbrellas for the creative-thinking strategies discussed in this book.

For example, negative brainstorming, a strategy we recommend, is a specific type of fluency. We pair each creative-thinking strategy with sample activities at different grade levels. Each activity shows how it can be taught using appropriate grade-level standards. As you read, we hope you find that you can teach creative thinking *within* the standards that you must cover. These are the two true objectives—teaching creative thinking and meeting standards requirements—of an effective education.

 ## Let's Think and Discuss

1. What is the biggest challenge you face in regards to teaching creative thinking in your classroom?

2. What obstacles have you encountered that keep you from incorporating creative thinking into your lessons?

3. What do you hope to achieve by learning about these creative-thinking strategies?

Chapter 3

# Strategies that Promote Fluency

**Creative Warm-Up**

Ask as many questions as you can about this picture, questions that cannot be answered just by looking at it. A poor question would be, "Is the clown on his hands and knees?" You can see from the picture that he is. Make your questions as different from each other as you can—don't just ask questions about the clown's clothes. Give yourself five minutes to think of as many questions as you can.

Fluency is the ability to think freely. To be a fluent reader, as all classroom teachers understand, one must be able to read with speed, accuracy, inflection, and excitement. To be a fluent thinker, one must freely produce an abundance of ideas.

Most creative thinking begins with generating ideas—lots and lots of them. The emphasis is on quantity, not quality, because the more ideas you have to work with, the better the chances of finding a solution. Some people refer to this action of generating ideas as "forced creativity." When students are freed from searching only for the "best" or "correct" answer, they become fluent with ideas (The Creativity Centre 2012). Their ideas flow from free-thinking, fast-moving thought processes. Students might generate the following answers to the creative warm-up. Any of these ideas could then be used for a writing activity based on the picture:

- Why did the clown decide to wear that outfit today?

- How come his mother let him get so close to the lake?

- Who does this clown look like in his family?

- What powers lie beneath the water that the clown wants to possess?

- What made the clown overcome his fear of the water?

- Is the water's reflection used to check his makeup?

Were you as fluent as this example?

Once the ideas are listed, careful analysis of the most useful ideas is necessary, but in the beginning, teachers should not worry about spelling, grammar, how words are used, or whether they are quality ideas.

Being fluent with ideas will help students once they enter the workforce. Companies need fluent thinkers to produce new products and improve their existing ones. Fluent thinkers are better problem solvers because they have the ability to generate ideas for improving processes and products (ITS 2012). Students should know why teachers want them to fluently produce ideas. But they need to understand that fluency is not making long lists for the sake of making long lists. Statistics tell us that the possibility of producing quality ideas will improve as the lists get longer (Ask the Inventors 2012). The more ideas we have, the better the chance we will produce something useful.

Under fluency, we have identified four strategies, all of which emphasize fluently generating ideas:

- brainstorming
- negative brainstorming
- SCAMPER
- attribute listing

The differences among these strategies are not as great as in later chapters, but they make an excellent introduction to the first phase of creative thinking.

## Brainstorming

Shawn Cirkiel, a renowned chef and owner of three restaurants in Austin, Texas, often brings his staff together to talk about food with the goal of creating a new dish. The most fun way to create new dishes, according to Cirkiel, is by tossing ideas back and forth with his staff. They first look to the market. If farmers have figs today, Cirkiel and his staff go back and forth talking about how they could use figs in a dish that evening. Perhaps there is blue cheese that needs to be eaten, so the conversation turns to ways to use blue cheese in a dish. Brainstorming is a team effort in this case. Once everyone's ideas are exhausted, the staff edits them to make the ideas streamlined and consistent. The idea for a dish has to function within the confines of the restaurant. The dish depends on the skill of the chef, the flow of the kitchen, and the ability of the servers to sell it to the customers. And based on what is available in the market, what is found in the refrigerator, and several ideas the staff presents, a perfect dish is born (Cirkiel, pers. comm.).

Effective brainstorming is a tool that helps people generate ideas for solving problems. Brainstorming can help businesses survive amongst competitors. It can aid both military generals as they look for new ways to fight wars and statespersons as they look for new ways to avoid wars. Such thinking ability is clearly useful to students, too. *What will be your topic for the science fair? What is the best way to solve this math problem? In what ways can we keep the peace between our feuding friends?*

Brainstorming can produce a lot of ideas. It is fluency at its best. The more ideas that are generated, regardless of quality, the better the chances of finding a solution. On the other hand, there will also be a lot of "bad" ideas produced in a brainstorming session. This is to be expected.

To begin, there needs to be something to brainstorm about. This should be based on a problem or the need for a solution. And this problem or need should be as focused as possible. For example, if an author is asked to brainstorm ideas for a new book, that is too broad to brainstorm. But if an author is asked for ideas for a story set in Egypt for middle school students, then the topic is focused enough to work with. The problem or need is narrowed down and the author has a better chance of producing a good idea for the book.

However, be aware of what hinders productive brainstorming. Placing students into groups to brainstorm can sometimes hinder productive ideas. Students might feel too intimidated to openly share with some students, especially if the other students are good at brainstorming. Also, the pressure that everyone expects great things of them can hinder their ability. But this doesn't mean that we shouldn't use groups when brainstorming. When we do use groups, it is important that students are placed with partners or in small groups where they feel comfortable sharing ideas. To achieve the most successful group brainstorming, students must first understand the rules for group brainstorming, which should be presented and discussed with the class before the session begins.

## Rules for Brainstorming

- Don't criticize the ideas of others. This breaks the flow of creative thinking.

- Think of as many ideas as you can.

- Don't edit ideas.

- Wild, funny, or even silly ideas are welcome. Sometimes these are the best ideas.

- Build on what others have to say. It is often the suggestions of others that bring a huge improvement.

- Keep a record of your ideas. You might want to return to what you were thinking.

- Begin to judge your suggestions only when you cannot think of any more ideas.

Initially, brainstorming should be done as a whole-class activity with the teacher demonstrating or modeling the process. Have sentence strips, sticky notes, or index cards available to record students' ideas as you brainstorm as a class. First, present a problem to the class. Ask the class to brainstorm solutions to the problem. Reinforce each student's ideas, regardless of quality—it's quantity that counts at this stage. Write ideas on sentence strips, sticky notes, or index cards. Remind students that you will not judge their ideas at this stage as the class brainstorms. Once enough ideas have been shared, it is then time to evaluate the ideas for quality. Show students how to evaluate these ideas into *good*, *better*, and *best* categories. You can tape the index cards, sticky notes, or sentence strips to the board, placing the ideas into these categories so that students can see your thinking. Change your mind as you evaluate these ideas, showing that the cards can be moved around the more you analyze them. At the end of this whole-class brainstorming, you should end up with only one or two ideas in the *best* category.

Then, have students brainstorm individually on sentence strips, sticky notes, or index cards. Encourage students to make long lists of ideas. When they have made adequate lists, divide students into pairs to evaluate each other's ideas. Partnering students might produce even more ideas, so allow time for students to share. Remind students that they should not judge their ideas during this time. Allow enough time for ideas to be written down. Next, allow students to form small groups or meet with new partners to share these ideas. More ideas can be added as students share with each other. Then, tell groups to place the ideas into the category of *good*, *better*, or *best*. Students should move their sentence strips, sticky notes, or index cards into these categories as they discuss them. By the end of the activity, only one or two ideas should remain in the *best* category. After a reasonable amount of time, tell the pairs to reveal the ideas they feel are most useful among those that they have placed in the *best* category. Finally, a solution can be chosen.

### Standards-Based Activity 1

**Mathematics Standard:** Uses whole number models (e.g., pattern blocks, tiles, or other manipulative materials) to represent problems

Place paper, pencils, and a variety of math manipulatives on student desks. Tell students they are going to brainstorm a list of ideas as a class. Remind them of the rules for group brainstorming. Then, write the number 5 on the board. Ask students how many ways they can show this number using the manipulatives. As students share answers aloud, write the ideas on index cards and tape them to the board. After a few minutes of brainstorming, tell students that they will now judge the ideas. Using student input, place each idea under the *good*, *better*, or *best* category. Repeat this activity using another number, but have students brainstorm individually on sentence strips, sticky notes, or index cards. Then, divide students into pairs. Have them share their ideas with partners and write down new ideas as they come to mind. Once time is up, have students categorize their ideas into the *good*, *better*, and *best* categories. Finally, have students share their best ideas with the class.

## Standards-Based Activity 2

**United States History Standard:** Understands the involvement of diverse groups in the civil rights movement

List the names of students whose birthdays are in a certain month. Tell the class that those students will not have recess today. Invite students to question this, and have them come up with ideas as to why it is unfair for students born in that month to not have recess. Write the ideas on the board. Then, ask students the following question: *Why is it unfair to discriminate?* Discuss and define the word *discrimination* (unfair treatment of one person or group, usually because of prejudice about race, culture, age, religion, or gender). Make sure they understand this definition. Then, have students give examples that they experienced or know from history. Next, ask students to talk about what they know about Martin Luther King Jr. Have them individually brainstorm activities the class might do to work toward the goals Dr. King was promoting. Then, have students share with partners, writing new ideas as they come to light. Finally, student partners should place their ideas into the *good*, *better,* and *best* categories. They should judge their ideas according to what is most practical to do. Their final ideas should be shared with the class and implemented if possible.

## Standards-Based Activity 3

**Language Arts Standard:** Writes business letters and letters of request and response (e.g., uses business letter format; states purpose of the letter; relates opinions, problems, requests, or compliments; uses precise vocabulary)

Show students the format for writing business letters. Read examples to students. Then, tell them that they will be writing business letters to real businesses. Spend a few minutes discussing the reasons people write business letters. Record these ideas on the board. (Reasons might include complaints, compliments, suggestions, or thank-you notes.) Next, tell students to think of businesses they could write letters to based on personal experiences and the reasons for the letters. For example, they could write to the doctor's office to complain about their long wait for their appointment. Give students sticky notes and tell them they will write one idea per sticky note. Give them time to individually brainstorm. Remind them that they should write one idea per sticky note and place it aside as they brainstorm. When time is up, have them form small groups and share their ideas. After sharing, have each group place its ideas in the *good*, *better*, and *best* categories. Finally, have groups work together to write letters to the businesses. Have students mail the letters and discuss any responses they receive.

## Negative Brainstorming

At times, we just run out of good ideas without ever finding the right idea for what we need. When this happens, it can be helpful to use negative brainstorming. Negative brainstorming encourages students to look for ways to make a problem *worse* with the goal of seeing the problem from new angles or viewpoints. The strategy is called *negative brainstorming* because students look for ways to amplify the problem instead of solving it. Instead of *How can we reduce littering?*, the question becomes *How can we increase littering?* Instead of *What is the best way to solve this equation?*, the question becomes *What is the worst way to solve this equation?* This new angle often reveals unexpected results, and students gain new perceptions because they are listing the exact causes of the problem. In turn, it makes them more fully aware of the problem and may spark an idea for a solution. This strategy often encourages a sense of humor and even silliness on the part of the participants. Creative ideas often spring from just joking around.

 ### Steps for Negative Brainstorming

1. Write the problem on the board or a large sheet of paper.

2. Have students individually list everything that could make the problem or situation worse.

3. Next, let students share their ideas in small groups and with the class.

4. As a class, look at each bad idea in reverse to see if a potential solution results.

## Standards-Based Activity 1

**Language Arts Standard:** Uses a variety of strategies to plan research

The following scenario demonstrates how a teacher implemented negative brainstorming. Notice how students respond with answers that are the opposite of what you would typically want. Encourage students to share these negative responses. This scenario can be easily adapted for any informational text.

Teacher:
*Today, we are going to prepare to write an opinion piece about the problem of tomb robbery in ancient Egypt. But we are going to try a new way of thinking about problems. It is called negative brainstorming. It has the same rules as brainstorming, except you try to think of really bad ideas instead of good ones. Remember, just as with brainstorming, there are no wrong answers! So, how could the Egyptians have buried their kings so that grave robbers would find them?*

Denise:
*Instead of making a mummy, could they put a table in the center of town and just lay the corpse out on it? In a few weeks, it would be a skeleton, and it could be buried in a small hole.*

Metrah:
*Could they cover the pyramids with a giant rainbow-colored cloth so no one would notice them?*

Mary Elyse:
*What if the burial chambers were made of pie? Then robbers wouldn't pay any attention to them!*

Trevor:
*Why not dig a shallow hole in the sand, put the dead pharaoh in it, and build a huge pyramid over him? You'd save the cost of a burial chamber, and nobody would ever bother him!*

Devin:
*Could you put beggar's clothes on the dead pharaoh, lay him out in a bare room, and store his fancy possessions in a secret room nearby? That would probably confuse a robber!*

Teacher:
*Your ideas are terrific! Your next step is to pick the question you are all going to research.*

Jennifer:
*Devin was kidding about beggar's clothes, but his idea about a hidden room full of the pharaoh's possessions, a secret room—that's a good plan. Maybe the whole chamber should be hidden. Should we see if they ever did that?*

Consequently, a rather silly idea gives birth to a researchable question, which will turn into a teachable writing activity.

**Mathematics Standard:** Uses a variety of strategies to understand problem-solving situations and processes (e.g., considers different strategies and approaches to a problem, restates problem from various perspectives)

Tell students that they will be using negative brainstorming to solve math story problems. Then, tell them that you have a certain number of quarters and four times as many pennies in your pocket. The total of these coins is $1.45. Explain that you do not want them to solve the problem yet. Instead, have students individually brainstorm a list of "bad methods" to solve this problem (i.e., What would be the worst way to go about solving this problem?). Give students time to brainstorm their lists. Then, have students share their lists with partners. Finally, have students share their ideas with the class. Review each idea, using negative brainstorming to see if a good method comes to mind for solving the problem. Remember, this is a two-step process. First, students enjoy the silliness of creating nonsensical ideas. Often, it is one of these ideas that sparks the thought for a useful solution. For example, students might suggest exchanging the coins for squashes, which may inspire someone else to put forth solving the problem using *x* for the amount of coins that they do not know. Another good answer might be to use a chart to find the right amount of coins. Then, have students implement one of the good methods and solve the problem. *(The answer is 5 quarters and 20 pennies.)* Negative brainstorming shows students what *not* to do, which by contrast makes good solutions more evident as students work through this strategy.

## SCAMPER

SCAMPER is a strategy used as an idea checklist that was created by Alex Osborn (1953). The acronym is as follows:

S for Substitute

C for Combine

A for Adapt

M for Magnify

P for Put to another use

E for Eliminate

R for Reverse or Rearrange

SCAMPER encourages students to think more fluently when generating ideas and is best used to broaden conceptual understanding of a topic or subject area. Again, it follows the notion that new ideas are modifications of those already in existence. Such fluent thinking often yields unique ideas that can be born from this strategy.

Among other things, SCAMPER can help students broaden their understanding of book characters, events, and people in history and can also help develop writing ideas and modify inventions. For example, if designing a prosthetic hand, students could apply SCAMPER to their ideas to help them come up with more effective ideas for how to design the hand.

**Substitute**—*Is there a way I can replace parts or materials from the original design with new ideas? Why would this help the design?*

**Magnify**—*Exaggerate one part of your design and explain what this does to increase its function.*

However, within certain content areas, SCAMPER, as described above, would be a difficult fit. For example, mathematical and scientific concepts may not need strategies that generate ideas. In these instances, SCAMPER is best used to broaden *conceptual* understanding of a topic or subject area. For example, if the goal is for students to understand the different kinds of triangles, a teacher could use these questions to help students explore what they know about triangles.

Students can use the SCAMPER strategy in various ways. First, the problem, challenge, idea, or goal that you want to accomplish should be defined. Then, sequentially work through the SCAMPER acronym to help generate ideas or use a few selected SCAMPER strategies. Remember, when planning these activities, you don't have to use all seven parts of the acronym. Select the ones that are the best fit for the content. Use Figure 3.1 as a guide to plan SCAMPER activities.

**Figure 3.1** SCAMPER Activity Guide

| SCAMPER | Defined | Questions to Ask | Key Words |
|---|---|---|---|
| Substitute | Is there a way to substitute something else for the product, process, or problem? Finding replacements can help you find new ideas. Anything can be changed. | Can I replace components? Can I swap materials or ingredients? Can I switch people? Can I change the rules? Is there another process I can use instead? Can it be renamed? | alternate, exchange, proxy, replacement, stand-in, swap, switch |
| Combine | How can parts of the product, process, or problem be combined to create something entirely new or different? Combining unrelated items helps you to expand your creative thinking. | Are there two parts of the problem that I could combine? Is there an unrelated component that I could integrate with this? How can I combine materials? What ideas can be merged? Can I combine it with other objects? How can I combine it with different talents to make it better? | amalgamate, blend, bring together, come together, join, merge, mingle, mix, unite |
| Adapt | Can you find a similar solution or change to your problem that already exists? Is there a way to borrow an idea and change it to make it your own? | In what ways can this be altered? How can I make this like something else? What can I borrow or copy? How can I change its function? Is there a way to use part of another element? How can this concept be adapted to another context? | adjust, alter, amend, bend, change, fit, modify, revise, rework, vary |

| SCAMPER | Defined | Questions to Ask | Key Words |
|---|---|---|---|
| Magnify | How can this idea be exaggerated? By magnifying the idea, you can discover new insights and find out why it is so important. | What can be made larger?<br><br>How can I increase it?<br><br>What can I do to exaggerate it?<br><br>How can I elaborate?<br><br>In what ways can it be made stronger?<br><br>How can I make it a bigger deal? | amplify, blow up, elaborate, enlarge, expand, increase in scale, strengthen |
| Put to another use | How can your product, idea, or problem fulfill a different kind of need? At times, we can find effective uses for our ideas when we think of new ways they can be used. | What else can I use this for?<br><br>How can this be used in an unusual way?<br><br>How would an animal use it?<br><br>How could a child use it?<br><br>How can this be used in a different context?<br><br>How could someone in a different country use it? | apply, bring into play, employ, exercise, harness, make use of, operate, utilize |
| Eliminate | How would eliminating the problem, idea, or product change the situation? When we trim our ideas down to the bare necessities, we discover the most important parts of it. | What can be made smaller?<br><br>How can I reduce it?<br><br>What can I do to minimize it?<br><br>In what ways can it be made weaker?<br><br>How can it be split into smaller parts?<br><br>How can this be understated? | abolish, curtail, diminish, eradicate, reduce to core functionality, reduce in scale, remove elements, shrink |
| Reverse or Rearrange | What would happen if the problem, idea, or situation were reversed or rearranged? Is there an unexpected benefit when it is done in a different order? | How can I exchange components?<br><br>Can I switch the positives and negatives about it?<br><br>What would result if I made it go backward?<br><br>What would result if I did the opposite?<br><br>Can I rearrange it to make a new pattern?<br><br>Can it be turned around? Down instead of up? Up instead of down? | change, contrary, converse, invert, opposite, reorder, reorganize, repeal, reshuffle, swap, transpose, turn around |

## Standards-Based Activity 1

**Language Arts Standard:** Knows setting, main characters, main events, sequence, narrator, and problems in stories

Have students read the fairytale story *The Little Mermaid* by Hans Christian Andersen and then complete the following questions as a class.

| SCAMPER | Question | Answer |
|---------|----------|--------|
| **S**<br>**Substitute** | Replace the setting of the story so that it is not under the sea. In what ways does this change the story? | |
| **C**<br>**Combine** | Combine the little mermaid and the sea witch. Describe this new character. | |
| **A**<br>**Adapt** | Imagine the little mermaid was a merman and the prince was a princess. How would this change the story? | |
| **M**<br>**Magnify** | The mermaid felt she had problems, but how could the problems have been worse for her? | |
| **P**<br>**Put to another use** | Pretend the mermaid did not drink the potion. How else could she have used the potion? | |
| **E**<br>**Eliminate** | What if the sea witch were not part of the story? How would this change the story? | |
| **R**<br>**Reverse or Rearrange** | What if the prince were the one who wanted to meet the mermaid? How would the story be different? | |

**Geography Standard:** Knows the physical components of Earth's atmosphere (e.g., weather and climate), lithosphere (e.g., landforms such as mountains, hills, plateaus, plains), hydrosphere (e.g., oceans, lakes, rivers), and biosphere (e.g., vegetation and biomes)

Have students individually select biomes to study for this activity. As they research their biomes, have them answer the questions to get them creatively interacting with their findings.

| SCAMPER | Question | Answer |
|---|---|---|
| **S**<br>**Substitute** | Substitute the average evening temperature with the average day temperature. How would this affect the species in your biome? | |
| **C**<br>**Combine** | Combine your biome with a friend's biome. In what ways is this combination impossible for the species in your biome? List at least three specifically. | |
| **A**<br>**Adapt** | Look at the amount of precipitation in your biome. Explain the positive and negative effects of more or less precipitation on three animal or plant species in your biome. | |
| **M**<br>**Magnify** | What if the temperature of your biome were to change severely? List and explain how three things would be affected. | |
| **P**<br>**Put to another use** | Imagine that no plant or animal life existed in your biome. What would be the best use of this land? | |
| **E**<br>**Eliminate** | Draw a simple food web that could be found in your particular biome. Take out one of the key carnivores. In what ways would this change the biome? | |
| **R**<br>**Reverse or Rearrange** | Look at one predator-prey relationship. Reverse this relationship. Why would this be impossible? Give at least two reasons. | |

# Attribute Listing

Attribute listing is another strategy for generating creative ideas. It involves dividing the problem or content into its key features, which are then addressed separately. Every time something creative is produced, it includes a new attribute that wasn't there before. For example, cell phones with touchscreens are much more convenient than cell phones that use cursors or roller balls to navigate. Listing *all* the important attributes of an object helps to be innovative. According to Frank Barron (1988), "the ability to change things is central to the creative process. New forms do not come from nothing, not for us humans at any rate; they come from prior forms, through mutations, whether unsought or invited. In a fundamental sense, there are no theories of creation; there are only accounts of the development of new forms from earlier forms" (83). In other words, nothing is new under the sun. It is only modified to look new. Attribute listing is one strategy that can help students creatively come up with this "modified new thing."

We describe the strategy of attribute listing in the following three ways:

1. **Listing ideas that describe a particular attribute.** (Students will list as many things as they can about the topic.) For the attributes of shapes, have students list as many different kinds of shapes as they can. Then, students can list as many different colors as they can. The goal might be to use unusual or different kinds of colored shapes in a mathematical picture.

2. **Modifying the attribute to look for possible ways to change it.** (Students will list as many changes to the topic as possible.) Have students list four main attributes of a character. Under each attribute, have students list ideas to replace that particular attribute and thus modify the character in some ways. The goal might be to make the character more interesting.

3. **Transferring the attribute to a new situation.** (Students will seek new and unexpected settings for the topic.) One example of this is using a current format to tell an old account. For example, students could use the format of *Diary of a Wimpy Kid* to write about an event from history, or students could use a talk show format to present information on transformations in math (flips, turns, and slides). Students can present information on forces and motion using a carnival format. The goal is to make the format of the presentation more creative and engaging than is typically assigned by the teacher.

---

### Standards-Based Activity 1

*Listing ideas that describe a particular attribute*

**Science Standard:** Knows that sedimentary, igneous, and metamorphic rocks contain evidence of the minerals, temperatures, and forces that created them

Tell students that they will be listing the ideas that describe a particular attribute with the goal of learning the details about the content. Divide the class into three groups and have each group make attribute lists of a different kind of rock (sedimentary, igneous, metamorphic). Categories may include what it looks like, what it feels like, what it smells like, or hardness. Encourage students to make long lists of these attributes with the goal of learning more details about the different kinds of rocks. Once the lists are complete, have each group share and combine their lists. Then, have each group share their lists with the class so that the others can learn about different rocks.

## Standards-Based Activity 2

*Modifying the attribute to look for possible ways to change it*

**Language Arts Standard:** Knows setting, main characters, main events, sequence, narrator, and problems in stories

Tell students that they will be modifying three different attributes from Judi Barrett's *Cloudy with a Chance of Meatballs* with the goal of creating a new story. Read the story and explain that the story needs some improvement. First, tell each student to make a list of foods not already mentioned in the story. Next, have students make lists of other places where this story could take place—the story is actually set in a fictional town called Chewandswallow. Finally, have students list other problems that could arise from the food in the story besides the weather going wild. When students have finished their lists, have them select key features from their lists to create a new story. Students can draw pictures of and tell about their story.

| Attributes List for *Cloudy with a Chance of Meatballs* by Judi Barrett | | |
|---|---|---|
| What are some foods *not* in the story? | Chewandswallow is the setting. What other settings can you think of? | What other problems could occur besides the weather? |
|  |  |  |
|  |  |  |
|  |  |  |
|  |  |  |
|  |  |  |

*Transferring the attribute to a new situation*

**World History Standard:** Understands the origins and impact of the plague

Divide and assign the following aspects of the plague to students so that every topic is covered:

- How the plague started

- How the plague spread across Eurasia and North Africa

- The impact of the plague on daily life in urban Southwest Asia

- The impact of the plague on daily life in urban Europe

- How Christian communities responded to the plague

- How Muslim communities responded to the plague

- How the plague changed the lives of survivors

Tell students that they will research their assigned information about the plague and then present a one- or two-minute newscast to the class. Encourage students to use props and primary sources and to dress the part. These newscasts can be presented live or taped. Be sure to have them perform in the order of the list for consistency.

 # Let's Think and Discuss

1. How can you fit brainstorming into your curriculum?

2. In what ways can negative brainstorming be implemented in your class?

3. What part of attribute listing do you plan to implement in some of your standards-based lessons?

Chapter

## 4

# *Strategies that Enhance Flexibility*

**Creative Warm-Up**

Take one minute to write down as many ways to meet new people as you can. Try to think of unusual techniques, such as landing a hot air balloon on someone's patio. See if you can make each idea *categorically* different from the others.

What does it mean to be *flexible*? Why does being flexible matter to creativity? Perhaps no one needs to be more flexible than actors performing improvisation. Think about it—two actors on a stage who have neither props, nor costumes, nor lines, and they must create a performance from nothing. One rule of improvisation is that both actors must agree with each other as the scene unfolds. For example, if one actor begins by saying, "We are in Egypt looking at pyramids," and the other actor says, "No, we are here on this stage," then the scene dies. Or if the second actor wants to be at a circus instead and says, "No, we are at a circus," then the scene dies. The inflexibility of the actors in this scenario makes the possibility of an entertaining, creative scene nearly impossible. To agree, the other actor could say, "Yes, and did you see the opening to the tomb over there?" The scene could unfold by painting these actors as tourists, grave robbers, or burial experts. By agreeing to be flexible and adding more information to what has already been said, the scene can take a very creative turn.

This may be an example of extreme flexibility, but it happens in day-to-day conversations, too. In his book *Improvised Dialogues: Emergence and Creativity in Conversation*, Dr. Keith Sawyer reveals the results of studying a Chicago improvisational theater group (2003). He found that what improv actors do on stage is mirrored in our daily conversations. We listen to and build from one another to create the conversation. His research shows that we are being creative when we have conversations, but we usually don't notice our creativity because it occurs so quickly and is often hidden. So even in our daily conversations, creativity is used in our willingness to be flexible, whether we do or do not recognize our conversational creativity. Let's explore a few ways that being flexible helps all of us.

**First, being flexible helps us be open to the world so that we can discover new things.** If we are not open to new things, we won't notice them. Discovering new things is exciting. This is particularly true in classrooms. Learning should be all about the joy of discovery. Many students are so fixated on getting the correct answers or earning good grades that they miss the joy of innovation, and in turn, true learning. Being flexible will help students make new connections across content, which ultimately is the desire of every educator.

**Second, being flexible helps us deal with change.** Don't feel discouraged if you are the type of person who doesn't like change. And don't fret when you have students who resist change. There are certain aspects of our lives where we can handle change and other aspects in which we don't like change. For example, I (Wendy) don't like change in my personal life. I am comfortable with familiar places, restaurants (yes, we go to the same Mexican restaurant every week), family, and friends. I like familiarity—don't ask me to try a new restaurant! On the other hand, my work must be filled constantly with change in order to keep me engaged and productive. Otherwise, I grow bored and become dissatisfied. So am I a flexible person? It depends. I *can* be flexible when I want to be. In the same way, we want our students to be open to change, even the slightest change. Using strategies that expand their flexibility will help students see the good in change.

**Third, flexibility helps us deal with failure.** It is very important that students understand how to handle defeat. Failure or lack of success teaches us what not to do. In 2012, the National Basketball Association's Oklahoma

City Thunder made it to the championship playoffs. They were a new team. Just three seasons before, they started the season 3–29. When asked about those three wins, Coach Scott Brooks said, "Even back then, we weren't losing games. I was telling the guys we were learning how to win games" (quoted in Latzke 2012). As mentioned in Chapter One, Thomas Edison understood that his lack of success actually taught him 2,000 ways to *not* make electric light. On the one hand, we want to teach students not to be afraid of failure. On the other hand, there is a healthy fear of failure. This fear is what drives us to work hard. In Silicon Valley, failure is not uncommon. A recent story on National Public Radio (2012) discussed technology startup companies and explained that for every success in Silicon Valley, there are countless failures. Joe Kraus, an investing partner at Google Ventures, funds these startups and sees the value in having a healthy fear of failure. He explains, "In my mind, the ones who have no fear of failure are merely the dreamers, and the dreamers don't build great companies. The people that walk the line between vision and being able to execute and having this healthy fear of failing that drives them—not paralyzes them, but drives them—to be more persistent, to work harder than the next person, that's a magic formula." Encourage students to see that failure is most productive when they view their work as experiments. They are learning how *not* to do something, just as Edison did.

**Fourth, being flexible also helps people see situations in their entirety, rather than as a group of uncoordinated details.** Flexibility is the ability to see how the parts work together to produce the whole. Being able to see all of the components in a problem and not just focusing on one of the parts is much more likely to produce a creative solution.

**Finally, in high-pressure situations, such as taking a test, most students seem to cling to the first idea that comes to mind without exploring or entertaining other ideas** (Dacey and Fiore 2000). Being flexible will help students resist this tendency. They will be more willing to question their first responses and search for better ones. Often, our first ideas are not our best, so helping students explore other possibilities is key to producing something more creative and beneficial.

We can learn to be flexible in certain areas of our lives and not in others, and that can be enough. If you cannot pinpoint any areas where you are flexible, try a new activity, such as a sport you've never played, to see if you like it or can even tolerate it. This will stretch you, and you will discover new things about yourself. In the same way, we can help our students learn to be more flexible a little bit at a time.

Another way to understand flexible thinking is to compare *vertical thinking* and *lateral thinking*. Vertical thinking is thought of as digging the same hole deeper to discover where the treasure (the solution to the problem) is buried. Lateral thinking is digging a brand new hole, and sometimes lots of them. Vertical thinking occurs when one solves a problem by going from one logical step to another (de Bono 1970). Lateral thinking comes from seeking solutions to problems through unconventional methods (Conklin 2006). Lateral thinking is a type of flexible thinking. Our brain is geared for vertical thinking, recognizing patterns, and following patterned ways of thinking. Practicing lateral thinking helps us break away from this habit and become flexible thinkers so that we can generate new ideas. Brainstorming is a type of lateral thinking. For the creative warm-up, how flexible were your ideas? One goal in doing the creative warm-up was to practice lateral thinking. The following answers are more predictable because they are the ones more likely to happen. We would categorize these lower on a creativity scale:

- In an elevator
- Online chat room
- Walking your dog
- At a bar

However, the following answers listed together would be considered more flexible and, therefore, more creative in comparison.

- Walking your cat
- Taking flying lessons
- Faking a motorcycle accident to meet a paramedic
- Leaving an unattended suitcase at the airport to meet a security officer

Figure 4.1 further compares vertical thinking and lateral thinking.

**Figure 4.1** Vertical Thinking and Lateral Thinking

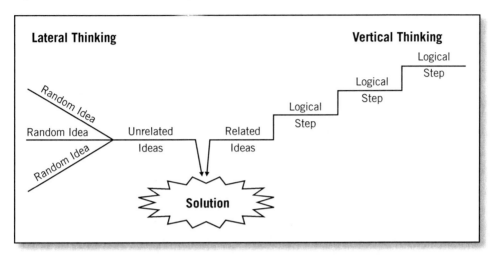

One strategy through which lateral thinking happens is the "creative pause." By *creative pause*, we mean allowing for what the Dacey Model refers to as incubation. This temporary break from the problem allows our minds to unconsciously seek solutions. We should not wait until we are out of ideas to take a break from writing. Instead, we should voluntarily stop from time to time as we may come up with better ideas than what we originally had. It is helpful to get up and walk around for a brief period. Follow this rule of taking breaks with students in your classroom, too. Talk with them about managing their creative ideas and why they need to take creative pauses. You may want to have a sign in the room stating, "Take a break—and THINK!"

A quick way to practice lateral thinking in language arts, for example, is by talking about movie genres—western, romance, science fiction, etc. Define the genres and give examples of movies for each genre. Ask students to dream up a plot for a movie they would want to see and have them adapt it for science fiction. After spending a few minutes getting started, instruct students to continue with the story but switch the genre to comedy. Let them write for a bit (there should be some giggles at this point), and then have them switch to tragedy. This can also be done visually by drawing pictures of a movie scene and changing the genre as mentioned.

Prompt lateral thinking by setting up provocations in order to encourage innovative thought patterns. By provocations, we mean anything that interrupts the normal flow of students' thinking. Habitual thought is disrupted. Unpredictable synapses may take place. Hence, unusual ideas are more likely to surface. For instance, explain to students that when you say "po" before a statement, it means that what you are saying is false. You are using this provocation in hopes of stimulating a new set of ideas for students to think about. Another provocation may be a reversal method. For instance, you may say "po" during your morning reading assignment, but you are writing math problems on the board. This may spark a conversation among the students about what they should really be doing. Say, "Po, it is time for the students to give me a test." Gradually, students recognize that these silly statements are invitations to come up with new, innovative ideas.

*Random input* is a separate strategy used to spark lateral thinking. Write a randomly selected word next to any paragraph you have written on the board. Tell students to try to make a connection between the paragraph and the word, seeing what they can come up with.

To get students warmed up for flexible thinking, you can use the ideas that follow. Look for any image, painting, or photograph. Primary sources typically work well for this. See Figure 4.2 for an example of a primary source.

**Figure 4.2** Molly Pitcher Primary Source

Display the image from Figure 4.2 and ask students to list all the possible topics that the subjects in the image could be discussing. Be sure to stress that you want *as many different kinds of topics* as they can think of, not just war topics. Encourage them to be creative and even list ideas of conversations that could occur today. After a few minutes, allow students to share their ideas with one another. How many of them expressed a variety of ideas about what is going on in the painting? The following is a list of excellently varied concepts that one student produced from the image. Notice how different the ideas are from one another. This is a great example of flexible thinking:

- scolding them for not doing the job right

- how bad the coffee was that morning

- the music in the background

- debating cars versus horses

- discussing their ugly uniforms

- the best cannons to buy

- what they had for dinner last night

- dropping their iPod® in horse manure

- how tired they are

Another way to get students to be more flexible thinkers is by starting each day with a puzzle question. To free students' ideas, do what professional improv performers often do before performing for an audience: ask the audience to stand up, hook their thumbs into their armpits, and walk around the room making clucking noises, bobbing their heads, and otherwise acting as though they were chickens. In the classroom, this will get students in a silly mood, which frees their minds to think laterally for this activity. Then, have students select partners to solve a puzzle question. You may want to pose the questions orally, as some answers to the questions may stem from how students hear and understand the question (e.g., in question six that follows, students may hear either a starry "night" or a "knight" in shining armor). Each pair must think of at least two answers to the question. Suggest that their discussions be in a whisper so that the other pairs can't hear what they are saying. The following are a few examples of these types of puzzle questions:

1. How many sides does a circle have?

2. A truck driver is going down a one-way street in the wrong direction. A policeman looks over and waves a good morning to him. Why?

3. Take two apples from five apples and what do you have?

4. What is brown when you stack it, red when you use it, and gray when you throw it away?

5. A farmer raises wheat in dry weather. What is raised in wet weather?

6. One night, a butcher, a baker, and a candlestick maker went into a castle. No one else was in there. When the group left the castle a few hours later, there were seven of them. How can this be?

When students have answered the problems, have each pair read their answers. Write short versions of their answers on the board. After all answers to each question have been given, have students vote for the best answer.

Possible answers given by students in the past include:

1. two sides—the inside and outside; unlimited sides; zero sides

2. The truck driver was walking; He is the policeman's best friend; It was nighttime; The policeman was looking into a mirror so driving down the one-way street looked like it was okay

3. You have what you have taken—2 apples; 5 apples because after you took them, you felt guilty and put them back

4. wooden logs; dirt; dead trees; pieces of brown plastic

5. an umbrella; the hood on his jacket so he doesn't get wet; animals that love water; fish in his pond

6. The last three—the butcher, the baker, and the candlestick maker— were pregnant women who gave birth while they were in the castle!

Another way to foster lateral, flexible thinking is the use of the "Six Thinking Hats." Make simple triangular hats out of six colors of paper, making enough hats for each student. In a class of twenty-four students, this means forming groups of four that have specific assignments based on the color of the hats. Suppose the job is to analyze a story the class has been reading. Each group's task depends on the color of the hats they are wearing. At the end, students should share their findings with the class.

**White hat** members answer questions *What information do we have? What information is missing? How are we going to get it?"*

**Red hat** members examine the feelings of the main characters.

**Yellow hat** members try to imagine positive and negative outcomes other than those presented in the story based on their reading.

**Green hat** members observe the work of other groups and try to improve their own group's work by thinking of even more original ideas. Students in this group wander from group to group, listening in on other groups' conversations and producing alternative ideas to the ones they've heard.

**Black hat** members listen to the ideas of the first four groups and use critical judgment to identify faulty thinking.

**Blue hat** members have the job of keeping track of the methods of problem solving that the other groups are using. Students in this group contribute by suggesting alternative strategies for creative thinking, which the other groups could use in future sessions. The more strategies you teach your students, the more productive this group is likely to be.

You can assign different tasks to any of the groups. The key to using these colored hats is that varying jobs purposely encourages different approaches to the end goal of thinking laterally. The "Six Thinking Hats" activity is designed to allow the thinkers to concentrate on only one type of thought, ultimately producing more information than if they simply had to answer a list of questions.

These are great activities to get students to become more comfortable with thinking flexibly and laterally. There are, however, some specific strategies that you can implement to encourage flexibility. These strategies include:

- Condensation
- Synectics
- Metaphorical Thinking
- The Williams Model

## Condensation

Striving to understand the essence or the core of a problem is what Jackson and Messick term "condensation" (1965). For example, you might teach students to build mind maps. Creating mind maps involves drawing lines between the significant elements in a problem in order to get at the most central element of the problem. First, construct a main attributes list. Then, draw lines indicating which ones are solidly linked. Figure 4.3 shows a sample mind map.

**Figure 4.3** Possible Causes of Being an Underachieving Child

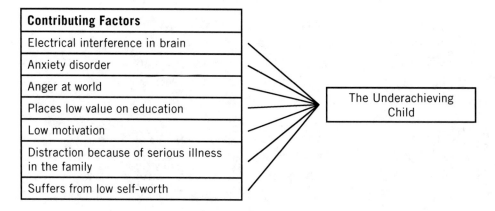

Figure 4.3 reflects some of the contributing factors of underachieving children. Building a mind map is a way to organize a "snapshot" of possible factors by creating a list of the elements that may play a role in shaping underachieving children. We know that the factors on the left often contribute to how likely a child is to achieve above or below his or her ability. But which factors are dominantly operating in your classroom? Which factors are the most essential? Only when you have mapped out as many *different* facets of this thorny dilemma can you approach a good answer. By systematically eliminating as many factors as you can, you begin to focus on the actual cause(s). In this case, only one factor (the first) is biological, and it is a rather remote factor. Most contributing factors are social causes. The mind map helps you to *condense* the many variables into a summary that you can more readily analyze. In this case, a psychologist would label most of the factors "intra-psychic." That means that most of the factors have to do with the child's self-image (Erikson 1963). This offers us a strong hypothesis, directing us where to start looking for a solution, and by a process of condensation, we can then narrow down our search for the central element of the problem.

One of the traits of creative people is their compulsion to discover this core. To condense a problem down to its simplest form, they often start with a spontaneous insight followed by painstaking reflections on the implications of their idea. An example is the Human Genome Project, an international research program that has identified the complete genetic pool of human beings (Collins and Jegalian 2012). The ultimate goal of this enormous data-gathering effort is to understand the essence of genetic inheritance. The Human Genome Project is the result of complex information expressed in a highly condensed form. As of yet, no one has made the giant leap that pulls all of these genetic insights into an explanation of life itself, but it is quite likely someone will.

Condensation always has the unusual power of summary. We usually think of a poem or a painting in this regard, but it is also true of the sciences. Perhaps the best example of this kind of thinking may be Einstein's famous formula that describes his theory of relativity, $E = mc^2$, which we earlier pointed to as an exemplar of extraordinary creativity. Physicists had long wondered about the total amount of energy in the universe, and numerous complex theories were offered. When Einstein discovered the answer, it was remarkably uncomplicated: *E*nergy equals all of the existing *m*ass of matter times a *c*onstant number squared. And what does this mean? Your authors have no idea, but it must be said that at least the formula is an amazing summary of a complex state of affairs!

Condensation is literally part of the art of sculpture. The goal of sculpting is to cut away extraneous material of the stone, clay, or marble. In carving a statue, the sculptor removes big chunks of extraneous material. When these individual pieces are gone, what is left is a broad image of a human figure or bust. Gradually, more of the remaining matter is cut away. If the sculptor is any good, what remains is the spirit of the person's body, or in the case of a bust sculpture, the spirit of the person's head and shoulders. Sculptors always seek this essence. The same is true of the art of literary analysis.

To apply condensation in a lesson, the idea is that students learn to think globally about a topic. They begin with details and move to a broad definition based on those details. The ultimate goal is to get as broad as possible with the final description. Teachers can begin by defining the main objective they want students to take away from the lesson, for example, *What does it mean to be two dimensional?* or *What does it mean to be a mammal?* Then, teachers should frame the question so that students will list many detailed answers. Encourage students to think of categorically different responses if possible. After a set time, have students summarize the lists. Finally, a broad, one-sentence description should be written.

## Standards-Based Activity 1

**Language Arts Standard:** Establishes and adjusts purposes for reading (e.g., to understand, interpret, enjoy, solve problems, predict outcomes, answer a specific question, form an opinion, skim for facts; to discover models for own writing)

As a class, identify all the major themes in Nathaniel Hawthorne's *The Scarlet Letter*. Then, discuss how those themes overlap and combine to form a summary of the novel's overall point. Having done this, have students produce a single sentence that collectively summarizes the novel's meaning. To direct students' focus, consider describing how the reader is expected to view Hester Prynne, the main character:

*Hester wears a mark of sin—the letter A for adulterer—because of the sin she committed. In doing so, she demonstrates the ways that punishment can affect human nature and sensitivity. The community sees her as a fallen woman, a failed soul who deserves to be disgraced for her behavior. As everyone struggles with their own moral choices, Hester has difficulty reconciling the symbolism of the A that she wears. In the end, the paradox is that Hester is rendered not the wild sinner that she is initially made out to be but instead a dull, drab woman.*

*Eventually, Hester's wearing of the A changes from the original meaning, and the community begins to view it positively as "Able" or "Angel." As Hester wears the letter, she becomes sympathetic to those who have been victimized by society, expressing a great deal of respect for the humanity of others. The Puritans, as time moves forward, view her not as the temptress that she may once have been but instead with a mix of sorrow and awe; in the end, she is revered by her community.*

As a class, have students summarize Hester's characterization. *Despite her sin, she is looked upon with awe, yet with reverence, too.*

## Standards-Based Activity 2

**Mathematics Standard:** Understands basic properties of figures (e.g., two- or three-dimensionality, symmetry, number of faces, type of angle)

Tell students that they will be condensing the information they know about two-dimensional shapes into a single truth that defines all two-dimensional shapes. Begin by asking students to list all the things they know about two-dimensional shapes. Encourage them to provide real examples, adjectives, and descriptions. List all of these on the board. Then, work with students to put some of these descriptions into a concise paragraph. Finally, have students write one sentence that describes two-dimensional shapes in their entirety.

## Synectics

Many creative solutions come about by using analogies. Velcro was invented because a man saw that his dog had a burr stuck in its fur. He took the burr out, examined it under a magnifying lens, and discovered that the burr had little hooks that caused it to stick to his dog's fur. He realized that a string of similar tiny hooks could be used to fasten clothing in place of zippers. Dr. Keith Sawyer, an associate professor of education and an adjunct professor of psychology at Washington University in St. Louis, explains, "We all have the ability to see the burr in the dog's fur, but the more creative person is able to make the connections more easily. Creative people are able to gain insight by forming an analogy between two things that seem really dissimilar" (quoted in Schoenherr 2006).

Synectics is a problem-solving technique that involves analogies. It is a way of bringing elements together in search of new ideas. Defined, synectics is "the joining together of different and apparently irrelevant elements" (Gordon and Poze 1980a, 1980b). The goal is to give students experience with thinking about analogies so they can use other analogies to make the problem-solving process effective. They will be making connections between seemingly unrelated items.

In the 1940s, a group at the Corning Glass Company was trying to think of ways to dispose of all the glass from the windows of old cars. They knew what to do with the metal and rubber, but the reinforced glass could not be made into new windows. The group generated many ideas for getting rid of the broken shards of glass, including dumping it in the ocean or throwing it down a mineshaft. All of the plans were expensive. One man in the group became bored with the conversation and began thinking about taking his son to the carnival later that night. He imagined all the things they would do, and for some reason, his mind fastened to the cotton candy machine. He couldn't stop picturing the hot liquid candy being sprayed on a spinning cylinder. Fooling around, he said, "I know. Let's melt the stuff and spray it around on a board, see if we get any pretty patterns." Some people chuckled, but someone else said, "Wait a minute—you might have something there! Maybe if we sprayed melted glass against a rotating cylinder, we could make sheets of the stuff. Any thickness we want. It would probably be tough but easily bendable. We could make things out of it. Let's give that a try!" Eventually the group invented fiberglass, which has proven useful in making boats, appliances, and car bodies. In no time, there were no more smashed up car windows to be had. They changed a costly expense—disposing of waste—into a moneymaker! The connection between the cotton candy machine and a fiberglass maker was the basis for the solution.

There are three types of analogies that synectics uses. When students practice making all three types of analogies, they are better prepared to solve problems. The three types include:

- direct analogies
- personal analogies
- symbolic analogies

**Direct analogies** allow students to look for comparisons between similar objects. For example, you could have students make lists of the similarities between campfires and stoves, or birds and airplanes. Once they start getting the hang of forming connections, they will eventually be able to answer the question *What things are like a stove?* By the end of this activity, you will notice students seeing more and more similarities between objects. Eventually, depending on the topic of study, you can tie in analogies to the lesson. If you are teaching about imperialism, for instance, you may ask students what animal is like imperialism. If you are teaching about inequalities, you may ask what situations are like inequalities.

**Personal analogies** ask students to actually *be* the analogy. You would have students describe the object they are being. If they are dogs, they may say, "I can feel my tail wagging." Next, have students list common emotions they might feel, such as, "I feel happy when I get my belly rubbed." Then, students should show even more insight into their lives, such as, "Sometimes I like it when my owner's friends come over, but other times they give me no attention and I hate it." Finally, by the end of the exercise, students should be thinking creatively enough to make the same type of empathetic connection with nonliving things. Examples include expressing the sadness of snow boots being put away for the summer, or a crayon crying because it had been dropped on the floor. Or students might empathize with a computer that is overjoyed because a bad writer has given up writing his or her awful novel on it.

**Symbolic analogy** is the most challenging type of analogy, forcing students to think of two opposite ideas at the same time. Students think of and write about such contradictory analogies as *dangerously friendly, powerfully inept, incredibly true,* and *significantly small.* Such mental exercises are often most productive in making creative products. You will get more insight into this approach when you read about minimizing and maximizing in Chapter Six.

---

### Standards-Based Activity 1

**Language Arts Standard:** Understands the basic concept of plot (e.g., main problem, conflict, resolution, cause and effect)

As a class, read *The Big Orange Splot* by Daniel Pinkwater and have students use the following analogies:

*Direct Analogy*

- How is the big orange splot both helpful and problematic?

*Personal Analogy*

- Be the orange splot. What advice would you give Mr. Plumbean as he wonders what to do about it?

*Symbolic Analogy*

- How is Mr. Plumbean's neighborhood a box of crayons?

## Standards-Based Activity 2

**Language Arts Standard:** Understands the effects of author's style and complex literary devices and techniques on the overall quality of a work

Have students use the following analogies as they read William Shakespeare's *Macbeth*:

*Direct Analogy*

- How can fair be foul and foul be fair?

- How can both heaven and hell be powerful?

*Personal Analogy*

- You are the dagger. What is your intention in appearing to Macbeth?

- You are the scorpion in Macbeth's mind. What are you doing in his mind? What are you telling him? Are you in control of his thinking?

*Symbolic Analogy*

- How is Macbeth a bird of prey to Macduff?

- Macbeth made these three observations about life. Explain each observation.

   1.  How is life an actor's brief appearance on stage?

   2.  How is life a candle that burns only for a short time?

   3.  How is life a candle lighting our way to bed?

## Metaphorical Thinking

Similar to an analogy, a metaphor is a word or phrase that by comparison stands for another word or phrase. Unlike an analogy, a metaphor is a direct comparison. It should not need explaining. If you were looking for a metaphor for a toothbrush, you might say that it is a tiny broom for sweeping your teeth clean. Similes are also included in metaphorical thinking, but they are always preceded by "like" or "as." For instance, "You are as beautiful as a sunny summer's day" is a simile. In metaphorical thinking, the aim is to identify what is similar between the two concepts. The poet Marianne Moore wished to evoke the harsh and gentle sides of a wild animal when she coined the phrase, "The lion's head looks like a ferocious chrysanthemum" (quoted in Siegelman 1990). This is a comparison between the lion's mane and a beautiful flower that has many lovely petals.

There is a relationship between the effective uses of metaphors and creative thinking. Using metaphorical thinking involves calling attention to similarities between two seemingly dissimilar things. A growing body of research shows support for metaphorical thinking. Howard Gardner, in his seminal *Art, Mind, and Brain: A Cognitive Approach to Creativity* (1984), describes talking to a group of youngsters at a seder, the meal many Jewish people eat to commemorate the flight of the Hebrews from Egypt. He told the children how, after a plague, the pharaoh's "heart was turned to stone." The children interpreted the metaphor in various ways, but only the older ones could understand the link between the physical universe (hard rocks) and psychological traits (stubborn, lack of feeling). Younger children are more apt to apply magical interpretations (God or a witch did it). Gardner suggests that the development of the understanding of metaphorical language is as sequential as the stages that Jean Piaget (1936) and Erik Erikson (1963) proposed and is closely related to the types of development treated in those two influential theories.

Examining children's use of metaphors, such as a bald man having a "barefoot head" or an elephant being seen as a "gas mask," Gardner and Winner found clear changes with age in the level of sophistication of metaphors (1986). Interestingly, two opposing features of metaphorical thinking appear as children develop: When you ask children to explain figures of speech, they steadily get better at it as they get older. This ability definitely increases as the child reaches the formal operational stage. However, young children seem to be the best at making up their own metaphors.

## Standards-Based Activity 1

**Science Standard:** Knows different ways in which living things can be grouped (e.g., plants/animals, bones/no bones, insects/spiders, live on land/live in water) and purposes of different groupings

What are the different types of groups within the animal kingdom? How do different phyla of animals interact with one another in their environment? Who gets along? Who doesn't, and why? Tell students that they will be given the identity of a certain animal group, including descriptions of each phylum. Review the definitions of the animal groups with the class. Then, assign students into one of these animal groups. Within each group, assign students a specific animal by handing each student a card with the name of one kind of animal within that group printed on it. For example, in the reptile group, give one student a card that says *crocodile.* Have students create metaphors for their animals. Then, have them discuss how their metaphors are similar or different from one another. Students can talk about if they are dangerous to one another, if they get along, etc.

At this point in the activity, students should create metaphors or similes that associate themselves with their group. "As cold as an amphibian" would be an example. The goal is for them to make an empathetic association so as to understand what distinguishes the lives and interactions of animals. Thus, they will learn the differences and similarities among the many different classes in the animal kingdom. Have students pretend they are the animals that are listed on their card and discuss why they are happy or unhappy with their animal grouping, which animal groups they might be scared of, or which group they would rather be a part of. For instance, one student may respond, "I am a snake. I slither around looking for prey. I really like that I am a predator to many other animals. It makes me feel somewhat safe and in control. I hope that I don't have to come across a crocodile, though. A crocodile is like a killing machine of the future—it could eat me!"

## The Williams Model

Frank Williams (1970, 1982) designed a model for creative behaviors, and the strategy chapters in this book are organized around the first four of these:

- fluency
- flexibility
- originality
- elaboration

The Williams Model also includes additional outcomes:

- curiosity
- risk taking
- complexity
- imagination

These eight student behaviors demonstrate students' creative thinking and are an extension of Bloom and Krathwohl's *creating* (formerly *synthesis*) levels of thinking (1956). Four levels (fluency, flexibility, originality, and elaboration) are cognitive, or intellectual, processes. Four levels (curiosity, risk taking, complexity, and imagination) are affective, or feeling, processes. But when students use any combination of the eight levels of this model, they are practicing and thereby increasing their ability to think flexibly. Teachers can form questions that support any number of Williams's proposed student outcomes instead of feeling that they must create questions to support all eight outcomes:

**Fluency**—Questions generate many ideas, related answers, or choices.

**Flexibility**—Questions encourage flexibility and seek to change everyday objects so that an array of categories is generated. Detours are taken, and sizes, shapes, quantities, time limits, requirements, objectives, or dimensions are varied.

**Originality**—Questions promote originality and seek new ideas by suggesting unusual twists to change content or to generate clever responses.

**Elaboration**—Questions expand, enlarge, enrich, or embellish possibilities that build on prior ideas or thoughts.

**Curiosity**—Questions promote curiosity and allow students to follow a hunch, question alternatives, ponder outcomes, and wonder about options.

**Risk taking**—Questions deal with the unknown by asking students to take chances, try new things, or experiment with new ideas.

**Complexity**—Questions create structure in an unstructured setting. They can also build a logical order in a given situation.

**Imagination**—Questions encourage imagination and help students visualize possibilities, build images in the mind, picture new objects, and reach beyond the practical limits.

---

### Standards-Based Activity 1

**Historical Understanding Standard:** Knows how to impose temporal structure on their historical narratives (e.g., working backward from some issue, problem, or event to explain its causes that arose from some beginning and developed through subsequent transformations over time)

Have students read the First Amendment to the United States Constitution: "Congress shall make no law respecting an establishment of religion, or prohibiting the free exercise thereof; or abridging the freedom of speech, or of the press; or the right of the people peaceably to assemble, and to petition the Government for a redress of grievances."

Then, have them interact with the amendment, answering each question that follows. Notice that complexity is not included in this list of questions. Teachers should not force complexity if it doesn't fit, and students should write only questions that come naturally.

**Fluency**—Why would a person want this amendment to be part of the Bill of Rights?

**Flexibility**—Why would a law-abiding citizen be against this amendment?

**Originality**—Rewrite this amendment in your own words to make it better. Explain why it is better written your way.

**Elaboration**—This amendment was written more than 200 years ago. What could have been happening at the time to make them include this amendment in the Bill of Rights? Defend your answer.

**Curiosity**—If you had to add something to this amendment to make it better, what would you add? Explain how this addition makes the amendment better.

**Risk taking**—What if this amendment were not in the Bill of Rights? How would this change the way we live today?

**Imagination**—Many citizens do not know what the First Amendment says. What could you do to make it easier for citizens to understand this amendment?

**Language Arts Standard:** Relates stories to personal experiences (e.g., events, characters, conflicts, themes)

Read Arnold Lobel's *Frog and Toad Are Friends* aloud to students and have them respond to the questions that follow:

**Fluency**—Toad found many buttons. What other kinds of buttons could he have found? Draw as many as you can.

**Flexibility**—What other two "creatures" could replace Frog and Toad? How would this make the story better?

**Originality**—Design a new swimsuit for Toad. How is it different from the one in the book?

**Elaboration**—Explain how Frog and Toad are different from each other.

**Curiosity**—How do you think Frog and Toad met? Act out how you think this happened.

**Risk taking**—What other story could you add to this book?

**Complexity**—What if Frog were the grouchy friend and Toad were the happy-go-lucky friend? How does this change the story?

**Imagination**—If you could write a letter to Frog or Toad, what would you say? How would this change the story?

## Let's Think and Discuss

1. In what ways do you (or can you) practice thinking flexibly?

2. Identify students who could benefit from flexible thinking. Explain why they would benefit.

3. Which strategy from this chapter can fit with a standards-based lesson that you have used with students in previous years or will need to use for the first time this year?

# Strategies that Encourage Originality

## Creative Warm-Up

The following test is known as the "Two-String Problem" (Landrum 1990). Your goal is to find a way for the boy to tie the two strings together.

As you can see from the drawing, the two strings are long enough to be tied, but they are too far apart for the boy to reach them both at the same time.

Some might say the most crucial trait of creative thinkers is *originality*. Originality refers to the ability to produce ideas that are different from what others can produce. It is valued because without original thinking, innovation would be at a standstill. Original thinkers are those who generate ideas that nobody else does. We know a product is original only because when we compare it to norms, we find that it is rare. This is the case whether the product is a painting, a building, a formula, a guitar solo, or a recipe. For example, take Salvador Dalí's painting *Crucifixion* shown in Figure 5.1. Metaphorical cubes support the body of Christ instead of the bloody nails in virtually all other ubiquitous portrayals of this seminal scene. Many art lovers gasp when they turn a corner and see it for the first time because they are shocked by the imagination behind this symbolic painting.

**Figure 5.1** Salvador Dalí's Crucifixion

Mihaly Csikszentmihalyi, author of several books about creativity, interviewed inventor Jacob Rainbow, owner of 326 patents (1996, 48–50). Rainbow, as quoted in Csikszentmihalyi's work, believes that original thinkers possess three qualities:

1. A large database of information

2. A willingness to engage in creative thinking

3. A willingness to produce and edit many ideas

**A Large Database of Information:** Without information, something creative cannot be produced. For example, Jimmy Page plays one of the greatest guitar solos of all time in "Stairway to Heaven." It would be next to impossible for Page to compose a solo like that without years of practice and an understanding of how to write music. He couldn't just decide one day to be creative with his guitar without knowing how to play it. It took him a lot of preparation beforehand. In the same way, we can't just decide one day that we will be creative in a particular area without sufficient preparation.

**A Willingness to Engage in Creative Thinking:** The person has to be willing and interested in doing the work. If Page did not care about writing a guitar solo, then his famous guitar solo would not be a part of that song. Page willingly engaged in the work of creativity.

**A Willingness to Produce and Edit Many Ideas:** It's a given that creative thinkers produce many ideas. But the majority of these ideas are not good ideas. Rainbow calls these ideas "junk" (1996, 49). Creative people don't effortlessly think of great ideas; they also produce a lot of junk that has to be evaluated to see if it is any good. For example, an idea can be deemed junk if its too complicated, if it has been done before, or if it could be done more easily. The original thinker needs to be able to discern whether it is good. Incidentally, Page actually recorded three different guitar solos for the song. He kept one of them for the final recording.

But how different is *originality*? As the old adage states, there is nothing new under the sun. That may be true, but there are certainly new combinations of ideas. It is not enough for a product to be new to its creator. The standard is that it must be new to a large group of people. And a truly original concept must have been unknown to everyone. The Wright brothers' airplane is a good example of this. Many of the principles of flight were previously known, but the Wrights were the first to put them all together in the form of a working machine. Today, we would consider a student creative when he or she produces an idea that has usefulness, is surprising, and couldn't have been known to the student before he or she produced it. Teachers can encourage originality in the classroom by formulating questions and activities designed to make students apply twists to change content or to generate clever responses. For example, a teacher might ask students to select an endangered animal and conduct research to find out what practices could help prevent their specific animal from becoming extinct. Once students complete this preparation stage and have sufficient information to work from, they can write a letter from the point of view of their chosen animal to a group of people or a company that is contributing to a problem that affects the animal or habitat. The following is one student's letter:

> Dear Women Who Use Too Much Hair Spray,
>
> The polar ice caps are melting. I don't see as many other bears as I used to. The temperature in Alaska is increasingly becoming warmer and warmer, causing the ice caps to melt. Without the ice I normally live on, it is hard for me to hunt the seals.
>
> Truly concerned for my future,
> P. Bear (AKA Polar Bear)

Even if students don't actually produce something original, your efforts have not failed. These strategies help *prepare* students for original thinking. Students need to gather information for their databases so that when an opportunity for originality comes along, they are ready. They also need to practice creative thinking so that they will eventually be able to produce something original. They need to understand that creative thinking is work. And they need to know how to judge their ideas and throw out the junk.

This chapter will show you innovative strategies for developing originality, including:

- visualization
- alternate uses
- creative dramatics

## Visualization

Visualization involves creating mental images of experiences, which can then be represented in words, pictures, or even formulas. In effect, students are making "mini movies" in their minds. While visualizing, students use all their senses and emotions based on their prior experiences.

Visualization is a skill that benefits students in several ways. It promotes learning because the mental pictures guide the learner to comprehension (WETA 2012). Visualization can also help students remember what they have learned because imagining images involves areas of the brain that are often less loaded with information, as compared to verbal material. It strengthens higher-level, divergent thinking because "[v]isual intelligence reflects a quality of creative problem solving that is characteristic of abstract thinking" (Barry 1997, 8). Most importantly, by learning to visualize, students gain a strategy that helps them assume control of their own learning in the future.

This strategy can be practiced through quick activities. For example, one third-grade teacher asked her students to close their eyes and said, "See a picture frame in your mind's eye. Make it tall and thin. Take a picture of this shape. Now imagine the frame growing sideways so that it gets wider and wider until all four sides are exactly the same length. Take a picture of this shape. Now let it get thin again, and imagine that someone came up and kicked it so that it leans to one side. Can you see it tilted? Take a picture of this shape." The students drew each of these three figures, named them, and listed their characteristics. Follow-up activities helped these students recognize the relationships among different quadrilaterals. Because this teacher knows that some learners visualize animations while others are more likely to see single pictures, she uses words to suggest both. For example, she might use the terms "grow" and "take a picture." As students work on this visualization in mixed ability groups, scaffolding is likely to occur as students share their experiences and benefit from those who can visualize well or differently.

Students can visualize through written accounts and therefore improve their writing. The following two stories demonstrate how well fourth graders can write when they have had even a little training in visualizing scenes. The teacher told us that the students' work was much more detailed than what they had previously produced, and she believed that the visualization exercises were responsible for the improvement. The samples that follow were written in response to the prompt, "Imagine that school is called off because of snow, so many kids gathered in the park to play. What are they wearing and what are they doing?"

## Student Response 1

My mom met me in the kitchen and said, "School's been cancelled because of snowfall last night."

Oh, it snowed again out here in Minnesota—that isn't surprising. But wait, did she say NO SCHOOL? YES! "Hey mom, I'm going to the park since there's no school, okay?"

"Watch for cars and be safe!" she replied as I bolted out the door.

When I got to the park, I saw lots of kids in all kinds of coats. Some coats were puffy, forcing their arms to rise horizontally as they waddled around. Other kids ran around in furry ones making them look like wild animals on the loose. Snow pants in all colors of the rainbow could be seen. And everyone wore black gloves, so if you lost one, you could never be quite sure if the one you found was yours. The kids were either making snow angels or snowmen. The snowmen eyes and mouths were made from rocks and the noses from sticks. But most kids were having a snowball fight! Watch out!

## Student Response 2

I was downstairs watching the news when I heard that school was cancelled. As snow poured down heavily, I breathed a sigh of relief because I had forgotten to do my homework.

Me and my friend Val pelted each other with cold, icy snowballs in the park. Even though the snow stung our faces, we still enjoyed our snowball fight.

Val was wearing a camo-colored hat that pointed upwards, a bright blue coat with black lining, and thick, grey snow pants. His gloves were pale orange with grey padding.

Visualization often involves creating mental images of experiences that can be viewed only in the mind. For example, most feelings, such as anger, and values, such as democracy, have no set visual depiction. Students can produce mental images of feelings they had while taking an imaginary trip to the sun, for instance. They might draw shapes and motions that show how they felt during parts of the trip. Because doing an abstract drawing rather than a representational drawing is likely to be outside their normal experience, they get practice in visual originality. They are also much more likely to remember the facts presented on the trip! The teacher can begin this mental journey by using the following prompt:

"Today, we are going to travel into space, first looking down on our school and then speeding above Earth past the moon, past two planets, and to the sun. In order to take this trip, you have to try your best to keep your eyes closed and really listen as I'm speaking. First, let's put on our space suits, which will protect us from the extremely hot and extremely cold temperatures of outer space. These suits are also equipped with jet rockets that allow us to travel at super speeds." (Continued in Appendix C.)

Figures 5.2, 5.3, and 5.4 show drawings created by students at different grade levels that are based on the visualization sun activity. These three drawings clearly demonstrate differences in maturity and likely gender. However, they also show that students are able to represent feelings in what are essentially abstract drawings. And this is an excellent way to help them learn the scientific facts they need to know.

**Figure 5.2** Third Grade Student Visualization Sample

By Owen, third grade

**Figure 5.3** Fifth Grade Student Visualization Sample

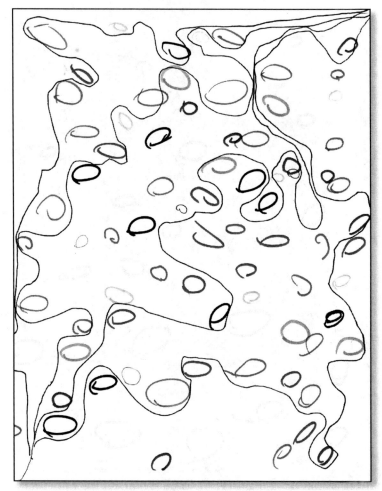

By Thomas, fifth grade

**Figure 5.4** Eighth Grade Student Visualization Sample

By Rose, eighth grade

## Standards-Based Activity 1

**Language Arts Standard:** Understands different messages conveyed through visual media (e.g., main ideas and supporting details; facts and opinions; main characters, setting, and sequence of events in visual narratives)

Tell students that they will be developing their visualization skills by drawing illustrations of a scene from a book that has no pictures, like a novel. Have them close their eyes and take a quick imaginary journey through the book that the class is reading. Tell students to select a scene they really like and let it play in their minds. Next, have students draw the scene as they viewed it in their minds. When students finish, hang the drawings on the walls of the classroom. Set up a gallery walk for students to see the different ways their classmates expressed the scene. Have each student read the portion of the story on which his or her picture is based to the class as they view his or her illustration. Discussing each picture will lead to a deeper understanding of what the book is trying to say as well as how the main characters, the setting, and the supporting details are depicted.

## Standards-Based Activity 2

**Science Standard:** Knows that models are often used to think about things that cannot be observed or investigated directly (e.g., processes that occur too slowly, too quickly, or on too small a scale, or that are too dangerous for direct observation)

Begin the visualization strategy by asking students to think about how the sun and the moon can affect how the sun's rays hit Earth. Show students the following diagram and ask what it indicates about the sunlight on Earth. If students have difficulty getting started, tell them that the circles represent the sun, the moon, and the Earth, respectively. What is the name for this phenomenon? *(solar eclipse)* How would this look for a lunar eclipse?

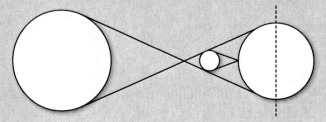

Psychologists have two concepts that apply to originality in the use of objects, which may come up a lot when you are in a jam. One is called *stimulus freedom* (Frankl 1985). That means you don't get stuck on one way of looking at the things that you experience. For example, if you are asked to do something that you don't want to do, you look for several interpretations of why you are being asked. You explore the possibilities rather than locking on to your first impression. That makes your reaction more adaptable and, thus, more likely to be successful.

An offshoot of this idea is called *functional freedom* (1985). This refers to the ability to see multiple uses for the objects you encounter. This is a creative trait because you don't always have access to the right tool for a job and will have to be inventive. This, too, increases your adaptability in the face of a problem you want to solve.

Remember the creative warm-up at the beginning of the chapter? Thinking of an alternate use for the mousetrap can be one way to solve the problem. Attach it to one of the strings, and then swing it away from you. Grasp the other string, catching the first string as the mousetrap swings back. Then, the two strings may be tied together. Many people are unable to reach this solution because they cannot imagine mousetraps being used for anything other than their usual function. Here's an example of what we mean: a graduate student in psychology studied the problem and said, "I've got it! I can use the mousetrap. I'll catch a bunch of mice until I get one that isn't seriously hurt. I'll make a pet of it, then train it to be a 'trapeze mouse.' Teach it to jump up on one of the strings and swing back and forth until it is able to swing over to me while I am holding the other string!" This is a good example of functional fixedness; the student believed that a mousetrap could only be used to capture mice. His solution could conceivably work, but it is much more complicated than simply using the trap as a weight.

One student in John Dacey's class, a young nun, attempted to solve the problem. She decided that the mousetrap was not really necessary. Lifting the apron of her religious habit (the long formal gowns of nuns), she seized the oversized rosary beads hanging from her belt. She swung them over her head while holding one of the strings. The beads caught onto the other string, and beaming with self-satisfaction, she tied the strings together while her classmates applauded!

People who have stimulus freedom and functional freedom enjoy the challenge of thorny problems. They know from past experience that they are likely to think of alternate ways to approach problems. Not all their ideas will work, but they are optimistic that sooner or later they will produce a good solution.

Here is an exercise students can try that calls for adapting how available materials can be used. If you asked students to list all the uses for a stone, they might reply:

- Build a wall
- Build a house
- Build a fireplace

Since these uses are what stones are intended for, the answers do not exhibit much adaptability. The following examples show answers that *do* exhibit adaptability. Pose the question in a way to garner more unusual answers, such as, "What are some *unusual* uses for a stone?"

- Use a stone to write on a sidewalk
- Use a stone to defend yourself if you are attacked
- Use a stone as a paperweight
- Crack a stone into pieces and use it for a puzzle to entertain little kids
- Estimate the stone's length in inches and use it as a ruler

- Use a stone to catch worms by putting the stone on a patch of ground, waiting two weeks, and picking it up to find lots of worms under it

The following are additional questions that can be posed to get students thinking of adaptability and alternate uses.

- Other than a screwdriver, what tools or items might you use to remove a screw from a piece of wood? *(pliers, table knife, nail clippers, etc.)*

- How could you cook a meal if you were stuck in a traffic jam in an evacuation? *(Place one of your hubcaps on the hot engine of your car, etc.)*

- How could you move a very heavy wooden box? *(Use a crow bar to inch it along; wedge round logs under it as rollers; attach it to a hot air balloon to make it lighter, etc.)*

- What would you use to start a fire if you were stuck in the woods during a snowstorm? *(Use only branches still on trees; tear off bark strips from white birch trees, which burn even when totally soaked, etc.)*

- What things can be used as weights? *(plastic baggies filled with water, a box of stones, a block of concrete, etc.)*

In a classroom, a teacher wants students to think about how a product, idea, or problem can fulfill a different kind of need. At times, we can find effective uses for ideas when we think of new ways to use the ideas. For example, a teacher could ask how the function $y = 5x + 2$ could be used in real life instead of simply graphing it. A student might answer that $y$ equals the amount of money that a student might earn babysitting the neighbor's kids, $x$ equals the number of hours worked, $5 is what the student gets paid per hour, and $2 is the tip. While doing this activity, students learn about functions and how they can be adapted to real-life problems. A teacher could ask how a character would view a problem in a positive way—for example, how Katniss

Everdeen from Suzanne Collins's *The Hunger Games* views her new life as a contestant in a positive way. If the class is studying murals painted on ancient Egyptian tombs, the teacher could ask for explanations describing the scene of the mural. With such exercises, students are broadening their understanding of the topics. Use the following questions to encourage students to think about alternate uses:

- What else can I use this for?

- How can this be used in an unusual way?

- How would an animal use it?

- How could a child use it?

- How can this be used in a different context?

- How could someone in a different country use it?

---

**Standards-Based Activity 1**

**Language Arts Standard:** Reads a variety of informational texts

Bring in a variety of pictures that show signs: street signs, airport signs, construction signs, etc. Then, take the class on a field trip through the school to look for other signs. Ask students what these signs mean. Then, select a few of the most unusual signs and tape images of each to the board. Ask students the following questions and list their ideas on the board next to each sign:

- What else could this sign be used for?

- How would a dog use this sign?

- How could this sign be used in an unusual way?

By asking these questions, students interact with signs, learning the meaning of these signs and how they can be misinterpreted or used in alternate ways. Finally, have students create their own signs, allowing other students to find alternate uses for the signs.

## Standards-Based Activity 2

**Thinking and Reasoning Standard:** Generates alternative courses of action and compares the possible consequences of each alternative

**Historical Understanding Standard:** Understands that historical accounts are subject to change based on newly uncovered records and interpretations

Display a copy of the primary source poster. (*Note:* Any primary source poster would work for this activity. However, be sure to know why the poster was originally created and any additional information that may be useful for the activity.)

Give students time to examine it. Tell students to write down several ideas as to why this poster may have been produced. Some students may notice the word *Berlin* as context for their ideas. After students have written down their ideas, tell them that it was created in 1918. Tell students to write down additional ideas of why this poster was created at that time. Some students may make the connection that World War I had just ended and use that as context. Finally, share the English translation: *Bolshevism brings war, unemployment, and starvation. Association to Fight Against Bolshevism.* (The Berlin address is given underneath.) Then, discuss why this poster was created. Students may need to research Bolshevism and why it was a concern in 1918. Next, discuss how Bolshevists may have felt about the poster. This discussion will help students look at alternate perspectives and broaden their thinking about how others perceive this visual image and the message it sends.

Creative dramatics—acting, miming, dancing, and singing—allows students to imagine not only with their minds, but also with their bodies. Students improve their creative problem-solving skills by incorporating play and imagination into the learning experience. Using creative dramatics also allows students to practice interpreting, organizing, and synthesizing ideas (Block 1997). Another benefit is that student comprehension of texts and understanding of material increase as a result of participating in activities that utilize creative dramatics (Harp 1988). These activities foster concentration, sensory awareness, self-control, vocabulary and language growth, and a sense of humor. Students have the opportunity to be different from their ordinary selves in a safe and nonjudgmental environment. They also have the opportunity to conquer stage fright, if they have it.

In creative dramatics, students perform as people, places, animals, or objects. The goal is to free the imagination. Creative dramatics activities may be divided into three stages: warm-up, dramatic activity, and debriefing. The warm-up allows students to prepare their brains and bodies for the activity, stretching muscles and thinking of topics to act out. To get a better understanding of the power of this strategy, consider the following interview with Janet Farnsworth, a creative dramatics teacher (Farnsworth, pers. comm. 2012).

**Would you tell us about your approach to creative dramatics?**

"Well, that's my life's work. I teach and attempt to foster *embodiment*. What I mean by *embodiment* is the idea that the body has its own mind. To access the language of the body, you have to quiet your 'verbal' mind. Children typically find this task much easier to accomplish than adults. By around age 10, kids begin to develop a sense of judgment from self and others. Inhibitions begin to develop. Letting go of 'What is everyone thinking about me?' thoughts gets harder and harder. The carefree laughter, dancing, and singing of childhood fades into a more questioning and analytical rhythm. To access more of their mental potential, I believe in encouraging children and adults to be expressive with their bodies."

**How can we apply these ideas to creative classroom experiences?**

"Take an example of a fourth-grade classroom studying the solar system. Ask the children, 'Who wants to be Mars?' Ask them to act as a planet would act. What does it feel like to be a planet? How does a planet move? What kinds of facts might people want to ask a planet? What kind of a sound does a planet make? As you can see, the list of ideas is lengthy. Expressive arts help the children to think on a different level than is typically taught in a classroom. It's a great way to stimulate the right side of the brain for more creative expression."

**How can teachers cultivate different forms of expression in their classrooms?**

"The most important thing a teacher can do is to discourage domination of the verbal mind by cultivating the nonverbal right hemisphere. I often teach dance to children and adults. One of the most important ideas when introducing dancing is to instruct the students to look only at the ground while they are dancing. That way, they do not make comparisons and aren't so concerned about what the others think of how well they dance. Worrying about judgment interferes with the normal language of the body. If my dance students are able to quiet the judgmental voice, we see their bodies' natural language emerge. Singing, dancing, acting, and miming all free the mind from its natural tendency to hear only the verbal voice. Create a free, safe, nonjudgmental classroom, and encourage students to get up, get active, let go, and let their bodies talk."

**Why do you think we are so concerned about the judgment of others?**

"Our society is all about self-judgment. We are constantly asking, 'Am I fit enough, pretty enough, skilled enough, young enough?' We spend a good deal of our lives wondering if we are okay according to some imaginary guideline. We can help to teach our children at a younger age that worrying about judgment is simply a waste of time and energy. By nature, I think children would rather have fun by moving their bodies. That in turn frees up their imaginations. Of course, later, they will need to watch each other in coordinated dancing, for example."

**Do you have any other ideas for how to facilitate expressive communication in adolescent classrooms?**

"I understand the challenges we as teachers face with trying to disinhibit children once they get a little older. Encourage a warm-up class discussion about what it feels like to be judged, how you feel toward those who are judging you, how you feel about yourself when you are judged by others, what the fear of judgment feels like. When they question one another, they will agree that everyone is in the same boat: fearful of being evaluated. Allow the children the freedom to then disinhibit. No one has to worry what anyone is thinking of them. It will be a new and freeing feeling. A teacher could ask the children to then pretend they are five-year-olds or animals. It's possible that in their mindset, they might be able to forget how judgmental they have become. Act, walk, and talk like a five-year-old or a baby colt. Have fun with it. Laugh, smile, giggle, and be silly. Get creative!"

There are effective ways to involve older students in creative dramatics activities. *Sociodrama* is a group problem-solving process with a twist. Developed by Ellis Paul Torrance, sociodrama is used to solve a group or a social problem by dramatic methods (Millar 1995). It builds on the group problem-solving approaches discussed earlier. Problems are presented in a deliberately contrived dramatic context. The individuals involved gather and decide on a problem, present it within a dramatic setting, assign roles, and then improvise a play. The leader, or "director," of the group has the task of guiding the sociodrama session toward possible solutions in an objective way, trying not to influence the outcome. The leader may use a variety of dramatic techniques before, during, and after a sociodrama session. The leader may also provide props, music, lights, decorations, all in an effort to create the right atmosphere so that the "actors" will identify with their characters and setting.

Creative dramatics can serve as effective morning warm-up activities. One activity involves walking in place under various conditions. For instance, students can practice walking through a building that is on fire, trudging through snow, or crawling in the desert. Another technique calls for students to act as objects that change forms. Whether they are rubber bands that keep stretching, flowers that are blooming, or ice cubes that are melting, students will be practicing creative thinking.

Once the warm-up is complete, students can try other creative dramatics activities. They can act as puppets, pretend they are playing tug-of-war, act like their favorite animal, or act like a human robot. Finally, students can practice sensory-awareness exercises. These exercises increase the awareness of the five senses. You may have them eat imaginary food or dance to imaginary music that only they can hear. You may also have students use their bodies to portray situations from a particular story. Overall, creative dramatics is a great way to enhance a student's creative thoughts and helps them understand others' emotions. Since originality is as much a matter of personality as intelligence, having this awareness is a great asset.

## Standards-Based Activity 1

**Language Arts Standard:** Uses descriptive and precise language that clarifies and enhances ideas

Tell students that they will be performing skits with partners. Divide students into pairs and distribute an orange to each pair, instructing each student to get to know the orange. Obtain a large paper bag, and have students blindly reach in and feel their orange, trying to notice any traits that make it memorable. Are there any remarkable bumps, especially on either end? Are there any nicks, crevices, or lines? Is there a small piece of the stem still attached?

Next, have students perform skits that answer the following questions about their oranges in a creative way:

- What is its history?

- How did it get to this classroom?

- What does it have to be proud of or ashamed of?

- What is its name?

- How did it get its name?

- What is its family like?

After students finish performing their skits, have them write different numbers on their oranges for identification purposes and place the oranges in the bag with a few other oranges. One by one, allow each student to blindly reach into the bag, trying to guess which orange belongs to his or her group. You may be surprised at how well students will do. Ask each student whether his or her skit helped in identifying the orange.

**World History Standard:** Understands significant individuals in the abolition movement

Assign students to act as different historical figures from the abolition movement. Historical figures may include Harriet Tubman, Sojourner Truth, the Grimké sisters, Lucretia Mott, Frederick Douglass, John Brown, or Olaudah Equiano. Allow students to research these individuals for homework. Emphasize the importance of knowing the person's views and experiences regarding the time in which the person lived.

The following day, tell students that they will portray their abolitionist in a gallery walk around the classroom. Their talk should portray that person's experiences and views. Divide the class into two groups—one to perform and one to observe. Set aside space for each actor. Allow the first group to perform while the other group walks around, viewing and interacting with the famous individuals. Then, have students switch roles.

As a final conclusion and assessment, have students write a paragraph that explains what they learned from this activity in regards to the abolition movement.

 Let's Think and Discuss

1. What strategy from this chapter will you implement first?

2. How do you envision this new strategy working with your content and students?

3. Which strategy do you think might be the most difficult to implement in your classroom? What steps can you take to ensure success when you use it in the classroom?

# Chapter 6

# Strategies that Develop Elaboration

## Creative Warm-Up

If you count the boxes in this figure, you will see that there are 8 boxes in the center—shaded and not touching the outside edge—and 16 on the outside edge, making a total of 24 boxes. Now, if you were to add 22 boxes to the center, how many boxes would there be in total?

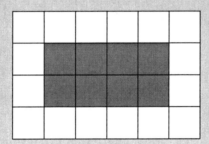

A sign of creativity is the ability to elaborate upon ideas. Elaboration in this sense is the broadening of ideas or concepts. It means paying painstaking attention to numerous parts or details for the purpose of embellishing them. This type of elaboration is not simply explaining details about something; it is the ability to fill in details when given a general scheme in order to make the idea richer, deeper, and broader.

Dr. Ellis Paul Torrance (1961) did a famous study on elaboration, the fourth aspect of creative thinking. He measured the creative abilities of first graders by asking them to elaborate on how three toys could be improved so that they would be more fun to play with. The toys included a fire truck (a boy's toy), a nurse's kit (a girl's toy), and a small stuffed dog (neutral at this age). On average, the students' scores broke down as would be expected:

- Boys' scores were higher than girls' scores for the fire truck.
- Girls' scores were superior to those of boys on the nurse's kit.
- The two sexes' scores were nearly equal for the stuffed dog.

Torrance administered the same test two years later to the same students when they were about to enter the third grade and had forgotten about the first study. The change was striking. Boys were superior to girls on all of the toys—even the nurse's kit! A number of explanations are possible. Perhaps girls simply become less creative with age. But this seems unlikely, especially over such a short period of time. Torrance concluded that "gender-role identification" was the cause. He suggested that elementary school teachers, most of whom are female, unconsciously suppressed girls' creativity by insisting that female students conform to a set of societal rules not required of boys (Millar 1995). He stated that one may often hear teachers ask for "some strong boys to help me," while girls are more likely to be praised for being "ladylike." Another teacher may say, "Oh, well, boys will be boys" when a male pupil misbehaves. This study suggests that even if parents of girls do not discourage creative imagination in their children, elementary school teachers might do so. However, more recent research reported by Dacey, Travers, and Fiore (2009) indicates that creative differences between the sexes are much less apparent than they used to be. For example, female middle-school-aged students in Spain "were significantly superior in *elaboration*" as observed in a recent study (Prieto et al. 2006, 286). It is entirely possible that the suppression of girls' ability to elaborate and think creatively no longer occurs in schools. The main point is that we strive to give students opportunities to elaborate so that they fully develop their creative strength.

There are many benefits of using strategies that develop the ability to elaborate. First, as students elaborate, they experience the "work" that creativity demands. Many people wrongly assume that creativity is some mysterious force instead of the result of intense, focused work. Students must be forced to work creatively. Deadlines and due dates are good for forcing creativity in all of us. Too many open-ended opportunities can kill creativity because creativity needs tension; constriction forces us to elaborate on a given topic. In Emmett Malloy's *The White Stripes: Under Great White Northern Lights* (2010), musician Jack White of the former White Stripes discusses this tension and constriction. White explains, "Inspiration and work ethic ride . . . right next to each other." He forces himself to work within a "box" because he knows that good things can come out of it. He is not always inspired to create music and often has to force himself to work. When it comes to writing music, he books a recording studio for only four or five days to record an entire album. His rationale is that giving himself "all the time in the world" to record an album kills his creativity. Deadlines and constrictions make him creative.

To expand on this idea of creativity as work, consider one assignment that required students to create a scale model of the major historical buildings and monuments in Washington, DC. This meant that their models had to be of correct proportional size and distance from each other. To comply, students had to consult various documents and maps to get building dimensions and accurate distances. Then, they had to convert these measurements to scale. After deciding on the dimensions, they began assembling their models and placed them on green paper, representing land, and blue paper, representing water. When the construction was complete, students wrote brief speeches about each building and monument that they delivered in a presentation. Instead of simply drawing a map and labeling landmarks, these students conducted painstaking research within the strict confines of the assignment to elaborate on the minute details of Washington, DC. Figure 6.1 shows one student's scale model.

**Figure 6.1** Scale Model of Washington, DC

When students are forced to elaborate, they in turn acquire a deeper understanding of the ideas and the ability to know whether they are moving in the right direction. One of our goals as educators is for our students to have those deeper understandings, which give students insights, and they can change course if necessary.

For example, if the objective of a unit is for students to learn the simple concepts of gravity and shock absorption, a teacher could challenge students to design an apparatus to protect an egg when it is dropped from a certain height. To encourage elaboration and creativity, restrict students to a set of supplies to choose from, such as three pieces of paper, four paper clips, two rubber bands, and five inches of adhesive tape. Next, pose a question that forces elaboration: "How many different ways can we construct this apparatus so that the egg will not break?" Groups get 20 minutes to build their first design. Each group then tests its apparatus by standing on a chair and dropping an egg. Record which structures work and which ones don't, and ask each group to reflect (elaborate) on why their structure worked or failed. This is when deeper understanding occurs, giving students the insight of "Are we moving in the right direction?" Have all students repeat the design process for improvements and retest. Finally, have each group define principles of shock absorption. For example, they may have rolled up each sheet of paper, taped them tightly, and fastened them to the egg in such a way as to protect it from cracking. Then, ask students to use their elaborative skills to imagine even stranger materials they could have used for their apparatus. Water? A vacuum? Grass? In a nutshell, students are encouraged to elaborate on their plans and to keep improving them by thinking of new, creative designs.

Another benefit of elaboration is that students learn to express ideas more concretely for others' understanding. What good are our ideas and creative work if others cannot understand and benefit from them? The elaboration process helps students work through the bumps and kinks so that the final product is clear to others.

Finally, good solutions are often found by elaborating upon ideas. As demonstrated through the egg apparatus project, elaboration helps students reach the best solutions. It takes constant revision and work to have the most creative products.

The strategies in this chapter are designed to develop students' abilities to elaborate. These strategies include:

- minimizing and maximizing
- spotting patterns
- substituting
- the Creative Problem-Solving Model
- the Wallas Model
- problem-based learning

## Minimizing and Maximizing

Good ideas often come from minimizing or maximizing a subject. A question that creative thinkers always seem to ask themselves is, "Would the solution to my problem be improved if I expanded or shortened it?" They look at the elements of their idea and think, "What if this were longer or shorter? Bigger or smaller? More or less complex? Increased or decreased?" Students need to be taught to revise and modify their work even when they think it is complete. As a teacher, you should constantly be asking students, "What can you do to make this better?"

Begin with minimizing. Minimizing means trimming a topic, object, or process down to what is absolutely necessary. It emphasizes eliminating superfluous elements, as opposed to the summary power accentuated in the process of condensation. This distinction is no doubt too subtle for many students, but we thought you should know it. Think of how music devices have grown much smaller in the past two decades. Look for opportunities in which students can analyze an item or object for the sake of minimizing it, such as modern-day improvements on products that we use. Students can test whether a subject can be minimized by asking the following questions:

- What things can be omitted?
- Can it be divided into parts?
- What would happen if it were smaller?
- Can it be condensed?
- What can I subtract?
- Can it be compacted?
- What can I delete?
- Can it be understated?
- What if it were miniature?

Maximizing, on the other hand, seeks to make the topic, object, or process larger, or magnified, with the assumption that bigger is always better. This is a key idea that advertisers use to make products seem more valuable to their audience, which could serve as a starting point in analyzing media and advertising. Students can test whether a subject can be maximized by asking the following questions:

- What does it look like when it is magnified?
- How can I exaggerate it?
- What extra features can I add?
- How can I make this stronger?
- What can I duplicate?
- What would make it more valuable?
- What can be extended?

## Standards-Based Activity 1

**Language Arts Standard:** Understands similarities and differences among a variety of media (e.g., ways in which documentary films, the Internet, and the radio present similar information; similar categories, such as news and feature stories in magazines, tabloid newspapers, and on television; literary elements in film and written stories)

Select a story for students to read that has also been made into a movie, such as *The Lorax* by Dr. Seuss or *The Tale of Despereaux* by Kate DiCamillo. Have students first read the story and then watch the movie. Divide students into groups of three. Begin by asking students if they noticed if any scenes that were included in the book were left out of the movie. Students should be looking for how the movie minimizes scenes in comparison to the book. Have each group make a list of observations. Next, have groups analyze how the movie maximizes scenes from the book. In other words, in what ways did the movie expand or embellish scenes from the book? Each group should make another list of the ways the movie maximizes scenes from the book.

Following the movie-book comparison, give students a simple picture book or have them select their own. Tell students to imagine that they are going to make a movie based on the book. They must think of things from the book that should be minimized or maximized. First, model how to use each question to make decisions about the movie adaptation. Then, have students use the questions to minimize and maximize, making lists of ways they can adapt the book for a movie.

**Engineering Education Standard:** Understands principles of aerodynamics (e.g., choosing angle of the wings of an aircraft, designing the shape and size of flaps on wings of an aircraft, choosing the aspect ratio of the wings of an aircraft, designing the shape of a model vehicle in order to minimize wind resistance)

Tell students that they will be learning about the basic laws of aerodynamics, including the lifting effects of air passing over a curved surface (the Bernoulli principle) and the roles played by weight, form, and the center of gravity on an aircraft. Inform them that they will design model planes that are constructed from quarter-inch foam board and must decide on the placement of tiny motors to move control surfaces (the rudder and elevator), radio switches to control the motors, and batteries to power both. These components need to be constructed and glued to the body of their planes so as to minimize wind resistance. If the wings are too small, they won't lift the plane, and if they are too big, they will make the model too heavy to be airborne. Students also need to discover how to maximize the flight performance of the planes by minimizing the overall weight of the plane (tiny batteries can only do so much).

Have students use the questions for maximizing and minimizing as they brainstorm ideas for their designs. If students are working in groups, have them discuss each idea before building. This discussion should help them with their final design. Direct students to consider how to create the best airlift with foam board, which snaps if bent too much. In the past, students have solved the airlift problem by gluing curved pieces to the bottom of the wings. When the glue sets, the wings curved from front to back, forming the perfect shape to achieve the Bernoulli effect of lift as air flowed more smoothly over the top of the wings. This created a vacuum and therefore a force of suction that lifted the plane.

## Spotting Patterns

In *How to Create a Mind* (2012), futurist Ray Kurzweil predicts that soon the distinction between the electronic brain (the computer) and the human brain (the cortex) will no longer exist. He predicts they will be combined because by pairing the skills in which each is superior, we will get a super-brain that is capable of solving the most complex problems. The computer tops the brain in two areas: the speed of processing data and the size of memory. Computers are more than 1,000 times faster. Because humans depend on evolution for change and computers depend on smart humans, the difference in the speed of the two is likely to increase exponentially. Google™ has been in the courts trying to obtain the legal right to scan every book ever written. Does anyone doubt they would be able to store this enormous amount of data on one computer if they chose?

Humans beat computers, however, in the extremely important realm of pattern recognition. In fact, some experts consider this skill to be the essence of intelligence (Bishop 2006). Computers are quite poor at it. For example, a program called "Captcha" protects websites from robot computers that try to imitate human respondents, usually to submit information automatically. This program, as many of us have surely experienced, requires users to type out a sequence of numbers and letters, such as *temPlAr3emot* with some of the letters distorted, when providing personal data. You can do it because you are a gifted pattern spotter, and the best computer is not. Young surgeons who frequently played video games in their youth are 40 percent less likely to commit a surgical error than those who did not play video games. This is partly due to the fact that playing video games provides extensive practice in the ability to spot prototypes quickly (Whitkin 2012).

## Standards-Based Activity 1

**Science Standard:** Knows that energy is a property of many substances (e.g., heat energy is in the disorderly motion of molecules and in radiation; chemical energy is in the arrangement of atoms; mechanical energy is in moving bodies or in elastically distorted shapes; electrical energy is in the attraction or repulsion between charges)

Obtain a hot plate or burner to boil a pan of water. When the water starts to boil, ask students if they can spot any patterns among the ascending bubbles. They will not be able to. Explain that there is no pattern because the motion of the molecules at the boiling point is "chaotic" and has no organized pattern as the bubbles stream to the top.

Now increase the heat, raising it until you can see six columns of bubbles forming. Explain that only at a certain temperature do the molecules begin to ascend in a distinct pattern. In fact, if you continue to raise the heat, the columns disappear and the water becomes chaotic once again. No one knows why this happens, but it is a demonstration of a fundamental fact of chaos theory: Complete randomness of motion never really exists (Gleick 2006). Ask students to explore other situations in which apparently random effects are not really random.

## Standards-Based Activity 2

**Mathematics Standard:** Understands basic properties of figures (e.g., two- or three-dimensionality, symmetry, number of faces, type of angle)

Tell students to imagine that the figure to the right represents a small marching band. The shaded center boxes—those not touching the outside edge—are the percussion instruments. The outside boxes indicate various kinds of wind and brass instruments.

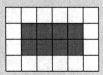

Explain that if they count the boxes in this diagram, they will see that there are 8 boxes in the center. These represent the percussion instruments, such as snare drums, bass drums, and xylophones. The 16 instruments that are on the outside edge are the wind and brass instruments, such as tubas, clarinets, and trumpets. The total number of instruments is 24. If you were to add 6 more percussion instruments to the center, how many wind and brass instruments would you need to add to keep the pattern? How many total boxes would there be?

Many students will simply draw the described set of boxes and count them to find the total. Some, however, will notice that for every 2 boxes that are added to the center, 4 are added to the total. Thus, there is a formula for any even number of additional boxes: N = original number of boxes + (number of additional boxes x 2). But don't tell them about this method yet!

Then ask, "How many total instruments would there be in the band if you added 18 wind instruments to the original number of 24?" Some students will now search for a formula that makes the calculation easier. Or you can prompt students to think of a formula. You can elaborate on this problem by adding additional shapes and patterns. For example:

Spotting patterns can also be used in language arts when analyzing the organization of writing or when analyzing the elements used by authors to write stories. In social studies, students can analyze patterns of immigration to understand the reasons for the movement of people across the world, or they can even analyze patterns of behaviors of leaders throughout history.

## Substituting

Substitution is the act of replacing one thing with something else to find a better solution. It is the same concept as Substitution found in the SCAMPER set of strategies discussed in Chapter Three. We can substitute materials, answers, places, people, ideas, conversations, ingredients, places, etc. Sometimes we may use the trial-and-error method until the right idea comes along. You may ask yourself, "Is there a different word, phrase, or formula I could use to better express myself? Is there a different medium I could use to express what I have learned? Is there a way to switch procedures?" The following questions can be used to help students practice substituting:

- Can I replace components?
- Can I swap materials?
- Can I switch people?
- Can I substitute the rules?
- Is there another process I can use instead?
- Can it be renamed?
- Can I substitute ingredients?
- Can I switch the parts?
- Can the place be substituted for somewhere else?

## Standards-Based Activity 1

**Language Arts Standard:** Understands elements of character development in literary works (e.g., differences between main and minor characters; character's point of view; stereotypical characters as opposed to fully developed characters; changes that characters undergo; the importance of a character's actions, motives, and appearance to plot and theme)

Have students read *Bud, Not Buddy* by Christopher Paul Curtis or any book with strong characters. Tell students that they will be using information from the story to create life-size versions of an assigned character, substituting words with art. Have students form small groups and trace the outline of a group member's body onto a large piece of paper and use the outline to illustrate an image of their character based on descriptions from the book. Without using written language, students should create their visuals by including at least 10 details about the character that are supported by textual evidence. Each group will present their characters to the rest of the class, showing how they substituted art in place of words.

Some of the important details about the central character, Bud, that one group illustrated were:

Bester: *He's African-American.*

Sam: *We put a rock in his hand with writing on it! Oh and a picture of his mother in his other hand.*

Abby: *We drew him with a sad face because he's an orphan and he doesn't know who his family is.*

Dianne: *We drew snow in the background because he's from Michigan.*

To extend this activity, have students illustrate another character, this time writing out the 10 details they illustrated. Next, have them illustrate an entirely new character, pulling information from the character details listed in different groups' lists. The point is to draw the character very differently from the way he or she is presented in the book. When finished, students should write brief articles on how the book would change if the made-up character actually were in the book.

## The Creative Problem-Solving Model

Alex Osborn, the founder of Creative Education Foundation, was the first to use Creative Problem Solving (CPS) (Treffinger, Isaken, and Stead-Dorval 2006). He believed that using identified steps when solving a problem can encourage creativity. The creative process is guided by these steps so that a creative, workable solution is produced. The idea is that creative and critical thinking work in harmony in CPS. He views both as complementary ways of thinking instead of polar opposites. Creative thinking works to generate as many ideas as possible; critical thinking works to focus thinking constructively, narrowing down ideas to arrive at a solution. He claims that effective problem solvers both generate and focus their ideas. In essence, "creativity requires constant shifting, blender pulses of both divergent thinking and convergent thinking, to combine new information with old and forgotten ideas. Highly creative people are very good at marshaling their brains into bilateral mode, and the more creative they are, the more they dual-activate" (Bronson and Merryman 2010).

The Creative Problem-Solving Model uses six steps to solve problems:

1. Mess finding (locating a problem to which to apply this model)

2. Fact finding (examining details and listing all known facts about a problem)

3. Problem finding (alternative ways to define the problem: "In what ways might we . . . ?")

4. Idea finding (divergent thinking; brainstorming for solutions)

5. Solution finding (convergent thinking; idea evaluation)

6. Acceptance finding (implementing the solution)

Over the past five decades, CPS has changed. It is no longer seen as a set of rigid steps that must be followed in a set order. The steps are flexible, allowing students to use them more naturally. These steps can be simplified into three main steps:

1. Understanding the problem

2. Generating ideas

3. Planning for action

## Understanding the problem

This step includes first identifying the problem and then finding out all the facts about that problem. It can take a good deal of time for research and analysis to really know what the problem is all about. This step includes *mess finding*, *fact finding*, and *problem finding*.

## Generating Ideas

This step involves the brainstorming part of creative problem solving. Students try to think of many varied and unusual possible solutions to the problem. All ideas are written down and taken seriously. Often, some very crazy solutions are given. Sometimes, these end up being the best solutions, so they should never be prematurely discarded during the brainstorming process. This step, called *idea finding*, should be free of evaluation, judgment, and criticism.

## Planning for Action

Planning for action is when a solution to the problem is identified and implemented. This is the time when the ideas from the previous step can be criticized and evaluated. To narrow down ideas, students can list what is good and what is bad about each of their ideas. This makes students analyze their ideas and think them through. *Solution finding* and *acceptance finding* are included in this step.

Students work with classmates to find solutions to problems. Teachers can facilitate small-group discussions and brainstorming sessions with very young students. By modeling and coaching students through CPS, students learn how to take responsibility for their own learning. The teacher's role is much like a coach's in the sense that he or she keeps students on task and helps them find the problem and generate many possible solutions.

Many of the benefits and reasons behind using CPS with students are similar to those of other problem-solving strategies. First and foremost, CPS helps students elaborate on problems with the goal of finding good solutions. It gives students a reason to struggle with purpose. It keeps them from jumping rashly to solutions. The end result of completing a task or assignment that was initially perceived as difficult builds confidence for future challenging tasks. Finally, the strategies that students use in Creative Problem Solving will benefit them their entire lives. By using CPS, teachers prepare their students for the workforce. Employers look for creative individuals with profitable ideas. Some of these students, with the proper training and encouragement, could become the next great inventors of our time. CPS gives students the opportunity to build "creative muscles." The more they practice creativity, the more their creative muscles grow.

Bronson and Merryman showcased a fifth-grade class that used CPS to investigate a problem (2010). The teacher presented students with the task of reducing noise in the school library, which had windows that faced a noisy, public space. Within this investigation, several key standards were met: Students studied how sound traveled through materials and gained an understanding of sound waves, they learned per-unit calculations as they worked with various materials to find an inexpensive way to fund the project, and they learned how to write persuasively. By the end of the year, standardized test scores rose, placing the school in the top three schools in the city, despite the fact that the poverty rate at this school was 42 percent.

Teachers can implement CPS by looking at key objectives from various content areas that need to be taught during the year. Then, they can form a problem that teaches this skill, concept, or generalization. At times, students will have ideas for real problems that they bring up in class discussions. Additionally, some great ideas come from storybooks. Teachers can read through part of the book, stopping when a problem is presented. Then, place students in groups of three, according to their specific needs. During the beginning stages of CPS, students will need to be guided through the steps. This may take place over several days. First, students must understand the problem. Next, students can generate ideas. Finally, students can make a plan for what they would do. Moving through the steps in three distinct segments gives students time to think about solutions. Finally, students can be assessed formatively and summatively. They can brainstorm in their journals before they start the problem, showing their ideas. They can write during the problem-solving process, demonstrating their thinking. Finally, they can write after they have solved the problem, showing how they arrived at the final solution. Students can even write persuasive letters—the possibilities are endless!

The goal is to provide students with opportunities to exercise their creative muscles. Teachers can do this by resisting the natural inclination to be the answer provider. For every question a student asks, ask another question that makes the student look for answers. The question can be as simple as, "What do you think?" This takes some practice and getting used to. Do not worry if you do not know the answers. There is strength in admitting you do not know something. Students respect honesty. Even as adults, we can learn valuable things from our students. We are lifelong learners, too, right?

## Standards-Based Activity 1

**Mathematics Standard:** Knows that an expression is a mathematical statement using numbers and symbols to represent relationships and real-world situations (e.g., equations and inequalities with or without variables)

Begin by explaining to students the problem that many people do not know the difference between algebraic expressions and algebraic equations. Tell students that they will work in groups and follow a set of three steps to create a game that teaches others about the differences between expressions and equations in algebra. This activity may take place over the course of a few days. First, tell students that they must take some time to understand the problem. This involves research on their part to discover the facts about expressions and equations, to understand why students get confused, and to determine how to teach others this concept. Give students time to work on each step of the assignment. Next, model how to generate ideas for their games using brainstorming techniques. Finally, help students plan for action as they come up with their best idea and implement it. The final day should include each group showing its game to the class as well as a time to reflect on what they have learned through this process.

## The Wallas Model

Think of the times you have been jogging, in the shower, or driving alone in your car. Suddenly, the answer to a problem pops into your head. You probably were not thinking about the problem at that moment, but an answer mysteriously came to you. You were away from the problem for enough time for your unconscious to work it out. Even when your problem-solving process does not seem to go through a rigid set of steps, chances are you are using what is known as the Wallas Model.

In 1926, Graham Wallas outlined a set of four stages to Creative Problem Solving in his book *The Art of Thought*. In order, these stages are (1) preparation, (2) incubation, (3) illumination, and (4) verification. Most of the time, the steps fall into this order. However, there are times when certain steps can be skipped or repeated as needed to find a suitable solution.

**Preparation** involves defining the problem. This is where every part of the problem is examined for full understanding and clarification. Relevant information can be gathered during this stage, including previous solutions to the problem that were not successful. Research materials can be collected in preparation for solving the problem.

The **incubation** stage is a reflection stage during which the idea incubates. Unconscious activity is taking place to help solve the problem. Some call this *fringe consciousness*, *off-consciousness*, or a *less-than-conscious* activity. Humans can only focus on one main activity at a time. Other activities can be done simultaneously, but they are done at lower levels of consciousness (Morgane 1970). For example, you can type an email while also listening to music. Listening to music is an activity that is done at a lower level of consciousness. You can walk, chew gum, and talk on the phone, but only one of these activities is the main focus. The problem-solving process works the same way. The problem can be unknowingly worked out at a lower level of consciousness as you focus on the main activity. At times, an activity can be completely unrelated to the problem at hand during this stage. However, incubation can also be a time of reflecting on the problem. Teachers should encourage students to always carry a pen and pad with them to write down ideas as they come. Having students leave the problem for a day or two may be a necessary step for this stage.

The third stage is the **illumination** stage. It is the "Aha!" moment. It is when the solution to the problem becomes clear. Usually it comes suddenly on the tail end of days or even weeks of incubation.

**Verification** is the fourth and final stage of the Wallas Model. It is characterized by checking to see if the solution is indeed the right one to the problem. If the problem is not solved, then the other steps can be repeated until a good solution is found.

Perhaps the most difficult stage of the Wallas Model is the incubation stage. This stage can be a struggle particularly for teachers who need to move through curriculum quickly. It takes time to allow ideas to come, and this can present scheduling problems for teachers. However, it is a worthwhile scheduling adjustment. Problem solving is a process that takes time. It is more important that students learn to struggle with problems instead of expecting immediate solutions, which are not always the best solutions. This prepares them for life outside school and for the future. The best way to deal with this dilemma in a classroom is to take a break from the project and do something else for a while. The next day, students can revisit the original project to see if some ideas have sparked in their minds. In effect, students will have spent time elaborating on both the problem and the solution by working through this problem-solving model.

### Standards-Based Activity 1

**Thinking and Reasoning Standard:** Identifies simple problems and possible solutions (e.g., ways to make something work better)

Read *Cinderella* to students and stop at the point where she meets her fairy godmother. Tell students to forget that Cinderella has this fairy godmother and they must find another way to help Cinderella meet the prince and live happily ever after without the use of magic. For the preparation stage, spend time talking about how Cinderella's life is very different from the prince's life. What would her limitations be in trying to meet the prince at the ball? For the incubation stage, tell students that they will spend a few days thinking about possible solutions to Cinderella's problem. Students should keep a journal with them to write down their ideas. Model for students how to select their best idea by using the brainstorming technique described in Chapter Three. Begin the illumination stage by dividing students into groups, giving each group a piece of paper to draw their best solutions. For the verification stage, have students share their drawings with the class and act out how they think Cinderella could meet the prince.

## Problem-Based Learning

Problem-based learning is a problem-solving strategy that engages students in solving a lifelike or real-life problem. This strategy is known for its group work, independent investigations, and inquiry. It values *meaning making* over *fact collecting* (Rhem 1998; Heitlin 2012). It is described as "a curriculum development and instructional system that simultaneously develops both problem-solving strategies and disciplinary knowledge bases and skills by placing students in the active role of problem solvers confronted with an ill-structured problem that mirrors real-world problems" (Finkle and Torp 1995). Problem-based learning gives students the opportunity to collaborate with classmates as they study the issues of a certain problem. Students can use the information they research to synthesize viable solutions. The amount of direct instruction in a problem-based classroom is very limited, so students have to take on the responsibility for their own learning. The teacher's role is much like that of a coach. The teacher presents the problematic situation, becomes the subject-matter expert, acts as a resource guide or consultant, and serves as a co-investigator who keeps students on task. Teachers ask questions like *Why?*, *What do you mean?*, and *How do you know that is true?* They question students' logic, give hints about erroneous reasoning, and model critical thinking so that students begin asking the same kinds of questions. The student's role is that of a participant who grapples with the complexity of the situation while investigating and resolving the problem from the inside out. Students see that the outcome of their work can make a real difference in society.

There are many reasons for using problem-based learning with students. First, we know that our minds are capable of thinking through complex situations, which promotes higher-level thinking skills. Research shows that it is the complex challenges that develop our intellect and ability to think productively (Caine and Caine 1997; Diamond and Hopson 1998). These types of problems do not provide just one right answer. Students are forced into thinking both critically and creatively as they seek to find solutions to problems.

Problem-based learning also increases motivation and builds confidence in students. Recently, professors have begun to restructure their course work around problem-based learning. They do this by taking the final exam and working backward to structure the course around a problem that teaches the key concepts they want their students to learn.

This type of learning provides opportunities for students to work with others, listen to one another, and synthesize information. While collaborating, great ideas can flow freely. Brainstorming with others brings out creative ideas that might not have been evident if students had been working alone. Problem-based learning is continuous brainstorming of what the problem is and how it can be solved.

Problem-based learning provides students the chance to develop strong work ethics. So much work, energy, and thinking go into solving problems. Strategies are generated for identifying and defining the problem, gathering information, analyzing data, and building and testing hypotheses.

Finally, problem-based learning is active. As students struggle to figure out a problem and apply what they are learning, they are more likely to remember the key concepts taught in that lesson.

A typical problem-based learning activity has several steps. These steps can be repeated as many times as necessary to reach a solution. The steps are as follows:

1. Locate a real-world problem that is aligned to learning standards and goals.
2. Determine facts and find a way for students to engage with the problem. Tie it to something that they are interested in. This is called the *hook*.
3. After the problem has been presented, expand on what students know about it.
4. Students analyze the problem, brainstorm ideas about the problem, and create an exact statement of the problem. This problem statement is the hypothesis. It may sound like, "How can we . . . in such a way that . . .?"
5. Students identify information necessary to understand the problem as well as resources to be used to gather new information.
6. Students find and share information by interviewing experts, collecting data, and conducting other forms of research. They may revise the problem statement and ask additional questions if necessary.

7. Students develop solutions by studying the information, finding a solution that fits best, and considering the consequences for each idea.

8. Students develop a presentation where they explain, apply, and justify their solution to the problem. Their information can be published and made available for others to see.

While problem-based learning is used predominantly in science classrooms, it can be used in any content area. It is important to remember that the problem should not have a fixed or formulaic solution. There is no one right answer. The problem is generally described as messy and complex in nature. It requires questioning, information gathering, and reflection. All these ideas require that students elaborate while they problem solve. Ideas for problem-based learning can come from sources like television, newspaper articles, and literature. Because students use prior knowledge to develop ideas and formulate them into a hypothesis, problem-based learning can be used with most any age group. Secondary students will invariably conduct deeper investigations with more complex results than elementary students will.

## Standards-Based Activity 1

**Health Standard:** Understands how eating properly can help to reduce health risks (in terms of anemia, dental health, osteoporosis, heart disease, cancer, malnutrition)

Prior to the activity, partner with a local preschool or elementary school. Then, present students with the following dilemma:

*Doctors around the world are concerned with the rapid increase of tooth decay in kids. It has always been widespread, but more recently, it has become prevalent in young preschool and elementary students. Doctors believe this situation is due in large part to the consumption of sugary junk food. They need your help in turning this problem around. How can you make a difference in your local community?*

Tell students that you are partnering with a local preschool or elementary school. Students will need to think about how they can inform both parents and students about this issue and help them to prevent tooth decay. Guide students through the steps listed in this section. As a final product, students may create picture books, videos, plays, commercials, or games to help advise students at this partner school.

## Standards-Based Activity 2

**Geography Standard:** Knows the ways in which the physical environment is stressed by human activities (e.g., changes in climate, air pollution, water pollution, expanding human settlement)

Obtain or write a letter addressed to the students from the principal concerning an environmental problem that the school is facing. This problem could be conservation of energy in the school, recycling, littering, or something else that is impacting the physical environment of the school. The letter should tell students that the principal is concerned that their school needs to do more to improve the environment in a positive way. There are practices in the school that do more harm to the environment than good. Close the letter by challenging students with the task of making a difference in the school. Use the steps in this section to guide students as they work to come to a solution to the problem. For example, students may organize after-school groups to clean up the campus, plan an event to spread the word, or utilize the morning announcements to draw attention to this. They should also implement their plans and measure the degree of success.

**Let's Think and Discuss**

1. What are two benefits your students will experience from elaboration strategies?

2. In what lessons can you incorporate the minimizing and maximizing strategy in your classroom?

3. How might you use the Creative Problem-Solving Model, the Wallas Model, or problem-based learning in your lessons?

# Chapter 7

# Ten Traits of Creative Students

## Creative Warm-Up

In a ring toss game, ten pegs are in a line stretching away from a player who tosses a ring ten times. The farther the peg is from the tossing line, the greater the number of points to earn from a successful toss. The pegs become progressively harder to hit. People who aim at the closest peg take a limited risk; if they successfully hit the closest peg all ten times, their maximum possible score is only ten (one point per peg). Those who aim at the tenth peg—the farthest peg—have one-tenth of the likelihood of scoring, so even though the tenth peg is worth ten points, they most likely score ten, too (one success is worth ten points).

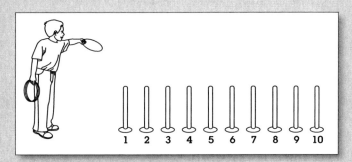

Can you guess which peg is the most logical peg to aim for? In mathematical terms, can you say why that peg is best? Can you explain what personality trait this reasoning illustrates, and why?

Research strongly supports the 10 traits described in this chapter that creative people possess: equitable gender values, courage, independent judgment, moderate risk taking, perseverance, preference for disorder, self-control, sense of humor, stimulus flexibility, and tolerance of ambiguity. Having an awareness of these traits makes us more likely to cultivate and practice creative thinking ourselves. Understanding them makes us more equipped to spot and reinforce these traits in our students.

You might ask, "What's the point in studying personality traits of creative people? Aren't these well fixed by the time a child goes to school?" There are some traits for which this is true. Eye and skin color, thickness of hair, birth defects, gender—these are a few human characteristics that are mainly determined by genes (Hunter and Mitchell 1997). Interestingly enough, running ability, left- or right-handedness, intelligence, and shyness are only partly genetic. These traits are also impacted by experience.

The ancient Greeks believed that creative ideas were gifts from the gods that were implanted in the mind by one of nine muses. For example, they believed the muse Erato provided them with poetic thoughts. Today, we believe that creativity is a combination of *biopsychosocial* factors. This means that creativity is the result of biological, psychological, and social factors. As you can see, psychological elements have been added. This view is superior to the long-held belief that all of human nature is created only through genetic and environmental processes. It offers a better solution to the old "nature vs. nurture" controversy. In this view, the following three interacting factors are involved in just about every human ability:

1. Biological elements range from the role our genes play in infant growth patterns to adult health issues. For example, some individuals have relatively complex neural pathways that are fixed at the moment of conception (Heylighen and Bollen 2012). This complexity makes such persons more likely to be creative because they can see more sides of a problem than can others.

2. Psychological elements include all aspects of cognitive and personality development. For instance, a child whose parent dies might become an excellent writer because of his or her drive to work out the confusion he or she felt from the loss.

**3.** Social elements involve such influences as family, school, peers, and culture. A child born into a family in which both parents highly value creative production stands an excellent chance of developing an imaginative mind.

Figure 7.1 offers examples of the biopsychosocial model's three components. The biological, psychological, and social components of this model all play a part in creative thinking.

**Figure 7.1** Examples of the Three Factors of the Biopsychosocial Model

| Biological | Psychological | Social |
|---|---|---|
| Fertilization | Personality | Maternal attachment |
| Pregnancy | Information processing | Sibling relationships |
| Right- or left-handedness | Problem solving | Success in school |
| Temperament | Motivation | Friendships |
| Physical development | Perceptual development | Media influences |
| Motor development | Language development | Medical interventions |
| Physical health | Moral development | Cultural stresses |
| Puberty | Self-efficacy | Marriage relationships |
| Menopause | Body image | Atmosphere in the workplace |

Schools can have minor influences on the biological factor. School breakfasts and lunches, temperature control of the building, and the school nurse can all impact creativity. After all, a student who is hungry, cold, or sick is not likely to be able to think creatively. Teachers can foster the psychological and social factors. Providing students with a psychologically safe environment and atmosphere where creative thinking is valued will have a major influence on the development of students' imaginative potential.

# Equitable Gender Values

Sadly, history has suggested a difference between the creative abilities of males and females (Piirto 1991). It was once thought that these differences were caused by brain differences—female brains simply lacked the "creative gene." Remember Torrance's experiment that tested elaborative skills in first-graders, asking them to elaborate on how they would improve a fire truck, a nurse's kit, and a stuffed animal? Torrance's study demonstrates the notion of inequitable gender values. As previously discussed, he believed that because most elementary school teachers are female, they unconsciously suppressed girls' creativity by insisting that female students conform to a set of societal rules not required of boys (Millar 1995). Thus, he found that the boys in his study were more creative, and indeed they may have been. Today, we have reason to believe that male and female gender roles no longer govern the creative behavior of the sexes so strongly. In fact, highly creative people are more likely to possess traits ascribed to both sexes (Piirto 1991). For instance, a creative person is often both sensitive and aggressive—characteristics traditionally attributed to females and males, respectively. The creative person is more likely to behave based on what he or she feels is correct and not what is expected or his or her gender. It has been shown that such persons are able to perform tasks that are not stereotypically gender-role based, such as a man picking up a crying baby. A man who would do this is someone who is not unduly concerned about what "looks right," and for that reason he is more likely to be creative.

The goal is to be gender neutral because neutrality promotes the search for the truly appropriate course of action, and as a result, this is more likely to cultivate creative thought. The following are ways by which you can support equitable gender values:

- Monitor your own behavior to see if there are feelings that conflict with this idea.

- Be on the lookout for students who display equitable gender values and reward them for it.

- Hold a discussion about what constitutes equitable gender values.

# Courage

Indira Gandhi was the daughter of the first prime minister of India, Mahatma Gandhi, a great pacifist and liberator. She was also elected prime minister of India for four terms in the time between 1966 and 1980. She was one of only a handful of women to hold high office at that time. These were extremely turbulent times in India, which included conflicts with Pakistan, building a nuclear weapons program, and the Sikh rebellions.

She was firmly convinced that the poverty-stricken rural country she governed would need to undergo many changes in order to bring it out of its status as a developing nation, and she pursued many innovative policies. Her imaginative ideas inevitably led to resistance by factions within India, but the courage it took to stand up for her beliefs in the face of numerous death threats was immeasureable. Out of office, however, she was imprisoned by the ruling party. Her arrest and long-running trial gained her great sympathy from many people. She continued to advocate for and promote her principles until her assassination in 1984.

Was Indira Gandhi the right leader for her country? There are many opinions on this. However, any governing individual in her position would have faced terrifying dangers. Was she scared for her life? She would have been deemed a most foolish person if she wasn't, and no one thought her a fool. She had such strong love for her country, however, that she was able to overcome the fear of potential danger in order to maintain and implement her plans. There can be no courage if there is no fear. Since most creative plans are initially received with some degree of animosity because they upset the apple cart, courage is required.

There are many examples of courage in which people have overcome their fears to achieve their goals. With your students, read stories that tell of the quest for courage. There are also a number of websites that inform parents and teachers how to cultivate virtues like courage in young children. For instance, Mary Lebeau recommends practicing the following five actions to help students develop courage (2012):

1. Talk about courage in class.

2. Role-play scenarios of courage.

3. Challenge students to act with valor in their daily lives.

4. Catch students behaving bravely, and reinforce the behavior with praise, especially in the presence of other students.

5. Allow students to grapple with difficult situations, which you may have to artificially create.

## Independent Judgment

A professor wanted to give a student a zero for his answer to a question on a physics exam. The student believed he should receive a perfect score. The question asked students to "Show how the height of a tall building can be determined with a barometer." The student's answer: "Take the barometer to the top of the building, attach a long string to it, lower the barometer to the street, bring it up, and measure the length of the string. The length is the height of the building."

It is an interesting answer, but should the student get credit for it? The student's answer did show one way to measure the building with a barometer, but it did not demonstrate his knowledge of physics. The professor gave the student an additional six minutes to answer the question with the disclaimer that the answer should demonstrate knowledge of physics. After five minutes, the student had not written anything. He had many answers to this problem—he was just thinking of the best one to write. His verbal answers are as follows:

"Take the barometer to the top of the building and lean over the edge of the roof. Drop the barometer, timing its fall with a stopwatch. Then, using the formula $S = 1/2 \ AT^2$, calculate the height of the building."

"You could take the barometer and begin to walk up the stairs. As you climb the stairs, you mark off the length of the barometer along the wall. You count the number of marks, and this will give you the height of the building in barometer units."

"You could take the barometer out on a sunny day and measure the height of the barometer, the length of its shadow, and the length of the shadow of the building. By the use of simple proportion, determine the height of the building."

"If you want a more sophisticated method, you can tie the barometer to the end of a string, swing it as a pendulum, and determine the value of $g$. From this, the height of the building can, in principle, be calculated. If you don't limit me to physics solutions for this problem, there are many other answers, such as taking the barometer to the basement and knocking on the superintendent's door. When the superintendent answers, you say, 'Mr. Superintendent, here I have a very fine barometer. If you will tell me the height of this building, I will give you this costly barometer.'"

Is this student a smart aleck, or does he demonstrate a valuable trait? Most experts would agree that he is an independent thinker. Independent thinkers are those who have the ability to process ideas and feelings without the supervision of authorities and without excessive concern for the judgment of others. He cares about being correct, not how he comes across to the professor. Creative thinkers demonstrate these traits.

Another anecdote tells of a seventh grader whose teacher asked her to suggest ways for students to get to school safely. She recommended that the local board of education sell the school property and physically replace the classroom with online lessons. This is not what the teacher was expecting, but her idea illustrates the mind of an independent, creative thinker.

As with most of the traits in this chapter, it is easy for students to be excessive in these behaviors. They can be too courageous or take more extreme risks. However, in the hurly-burly of the classroom and the need to maintain order, our tendency may be to suppress independent judgment. It is important to recognize and appreciate this independent judgment when it shows up in our students. If every student were exercising independent judgment, of course, things would be chaotic. But there is such a thing as "controlled chaos." Allowing students to have some control over decisions through open-ended tasks allows for independent judgment to be exercised by students. For example, instead of assigning a group project on the role of economics in the Great War, ask groups to select factors that played a role in the war and then analyze them. This method is more open-ended and fosters independent thinking. When working in groups, teachers can establish guidelines and parameters for these small groups and allow students to exercise independent judgment as they work together. When students express independent judgment with nonconforming answers, their ideas are typically creative and unusual. Just being aware of what independent judgment looks like when it shows up in our students can keep teachers from jumping to conclusions about students' behavior. Can you see how this also promotes creativity?

## Moderate Risk Taking

Remember the creative warm-up at the beginning of this chapter? The likely scores for the nearest and farthest pegs are the same: 10. Those willing to take a moderate risk would most likely aim at the fifth or sixth peg. For those two pegs, the likely score would be 30 (six successes multiplied by five points for peg #5, or five successes multiplied by six points for peg #6). Obviously these figures only hold true for this particular game, but they are representative of the real world. Those who take either small risks or huge risks are less likely to be successful in their endeavors than those who take moderate risks. Successful people are those who know how to identify a moderate risk and then confidently take it. Unfortunately, we often socialize our children in ways that discourage sensible risk taking and may even cause them to be risk-averse (Sternberg and Lubart 1995). Contact with germs serves as a good analogy here. Many parents do everything in their power to ensure their children's cleanliness. However, children who live in sterile environments are vulnerable to infection because they haven't built up adequate immunities. Kids *need* to get dirty sometimes. We also need to let them take moderate risks. How do they learn to do this? Practice. Only through making many judgments can they become aware of how risky things can be and also how risk can be handled well.

Moderate risk taking is key to enhancing students' creativity. If students never do anything challenging or hard, they won't be stretched. Taking risks is scary. You may have heard the saying, "If I don't get up, then I can't fall down." British singer Natasha Bedingfield (2010) wrote a song along that line titled "Can't Fall Down." The lyrics demonstrate this point and shows both her fear of and longing for taking a risk.

And the higher you go, the harder you fall
If I want to be safe, then I just stay small
Wanna grow to the sky where it's beautiful
But I can't see that from the forest floor
…Cause if I don't get up, then I can't fall down.

Taking on challenges puts students in situations where they must grow. And when they achieve these goals that they first believed were too difficult, their sense of satisfaction and accomplishment grows (Csikszentmihalyi 1996).

What determines a child's risk-taking capacity? To a certain degree, it is genetics. Some children seem to seek out scary experiences, such as riding on roller coasters. They explore and expand, and when disaster strikes, they may be dazed but rarely daunted. Other children are more cautious by nature, hesitant to venture into unfamiliar territory; they want to preview the script before accepting the part. This is why it is so important to support students through inevitable periods of failure or rejection.

Provide opportunities for risk in your classroom, encouraging all students to push themselves to take chances. Praise effort, not necessarily success. With students who are particularly risk-averse, hold discussions with the aim of providing insights into what is holding them back. Practice breeds success, while lack of practice encourages fear.

# Perseverance

Why are some students so persistent in the pursuit of their goals while others find it so hard to persevere? Those who struggle seem to "hit a wall." There are many factors, but the difference amounts to one value—desire. Even highly anxious children will pursue their goals when the drive to achieve is strong enough.

Unfortunately, anxious children quite often lose their desire to achieve and persevere because of the need to protect themselves from becoming frightened. Fear of fear itself overwhelms their zeal for progress.

Gradually these students lose their drive. Without realizing it, they begin to drift into self-defeating thoughts. Before they know it, they have lost faith in their goal and themselves. It is no wonder they are incapable of creative thinking. They are too worried about failing to be productive and creative. However, most of them have an asset that they fail to realize—their own creative imaginations. Ironically, anxious students are often the most *potentially* creative ones. That is why they are anxious—they can imagine scary circumstances that the others cannot imagine. As personally observed by Dacey in his psychotherapy practice, youth with anxiety disorders can be taught to use their vivid imaginations positively. They can learn to channel fear into creative solutions that help them persevere in their struggles.

You can help students experience perseverance by describing clear, rewarding objectives for them to meet. For example, you could ask them to find an interesting anecdote or joke that they could describe in class. Then, you could ask who would rather not participate. Work with these "quitters" to think of alternative ways that they can overcome their stage fright and persevere. They may want to record themselves telling a joke, or they may want to write their anecdote on the board. When they experience a positive response from their classmates, they will become more likely to persevere against their fears in the future. For an extensive discussion of this subject, see Dacey and Fiore (2000) and Dacey and Weygint (2002).

# Preference for Disorder

Look at the drawings. These drawings are facsimiles of the Welsh Figure Preference Test (Welsh 2012).

Some drawings are complex while others are simple. Some drawings are sparse and even while others are more intricate. Some are symmetrical while others are asymmetrical. When asked to choose between a pair of drawings, more creative individuals tend to choose more drawings from the right, more disordered column. They do so because they tend to prefer the challenge of disorder. Imaginative people often like complex concepts over simple ones. Anarchy is an interesting concept to them because they enjoy the tough task of creating order out of disorder. For creative individuals, the richness of disorder arouses more curiosity than the normality of simplicity. They are intrigued by the unusual. Being in control of resolving disorder gives creative people the ultimate sense of triumph (Barron 1988).

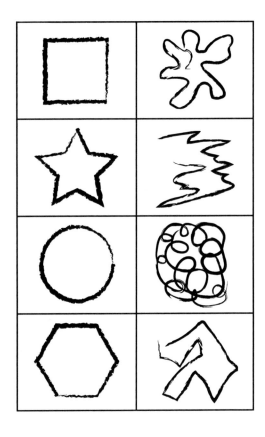

One way to encourage positive encounters with disorder is to maintain a "creativity place" that includes a wide variety of items like blocks, marbles, ribbons, stones, and colored shapes. Invite students to stop by from time to time and arrange the materials into interesting shapes. Encourage them to write their names on sheets of paper next to their assemblage. Notice whether there are any new offerings at the end of the day. Discuss these creations and the imagination it took to create them. An excellent discussion of this idea appears in Heard and McDonough (2009).

# Self-Control

In order to relate the importance of self-control to creativity, we must first define it. Self-control is "a set of cognitive and attitudinal skills that may be learned throughout the lifetime. These skills permit people to do (or not do) what they wish—even when it is not easy" (Tucker-Ladd 2004).

Many individuals believe that creative people tend to be wild, spontaneous, and impulsive. Perhaps this stereotype stems from the media's portrayal of artists and scientists as careless or peculiar. And this portrayal may describe some highly gifted individuals. However, it is important to realize that more often than not, this stereotype is quite inaccurate (Dacey and Packer 1992). For instance, it is hard to believe that Bill Gates was wild and impulsive when he set out to plan Microsoft®. In order to accomplish something of such magnitude, much discipline and analysis is necessary. The quality that motivates such a process is known as *self-control*. We might not all exhibit the *extraordinary* creativity of Bill Gates, but we can learn from those who do and apply their example to our lives.

Research shows that highly inventive adolescents show high levels of self-control (Dacey 1989a, 1989b, and 1989c). A symbiotic relationship exists between creativity and self-control. One needs creativity in order to conceive of a plan or visualize a desired outcome. Both of these elements are essential to self-control. One also needs self-control in order to use time wisely, work diligently, and have the perseverance to fully develop creative products.

Deane Shapiro et al. developed a model of self-control that examines how choosing a certain plan may result in one of four outcomes (Shapiro et al. 2010). The four outcomes of Shapiro's model are shown in Figure 7.2.

**Figure 7.2** Shapiro's Model of Self-Control

|  | Assertion | Yielding |
|---|---|---|
| **Positive** | 1. active control, positive assertion | 2. relinquishing control, positive yielding |
| **Negative** | 3. overcontrol, negative assertion | 4. too little control, negative yielding |

The first outcome is the result of active control and positive assertion. Planning to work out for an hour per day and sticking to this plan fits this description. The second outcome that Shapiro et al. describe is the result of relinquishing control and positively yielding to another individual. The person in this situation accepts control by another. For example, allowing a surgeon to operate on you fits this description. The third outcome results from too much control (overcontrol) combined with negative assertion. The person in this situation exercises an excessive amount of control without taking any positive action. For example, having an eating disorder fits this description. Enormous self-control is required but to negative ends. The final outcome results from too little control and negative yielding. An alcoholic who refuses to get help would be an example.

Self-control can be taught. The first step toward teaching self-control is realizing that it is not an inborn trait. People learn to postpone gratification in order to get greater rewards in the future. Some learn it better than others. Set up a reinforcement system in your classroom where students can earn small rewards immediately after making accomplishments or bigger rewards if they wait until they string together a series of accomplishments. This can be as simple as turning in work on time or learning to keep their hands to themselves. There is nothing mysterious about self-control. Whether it is asserting or yielding, students learn to control themselves because it pays off to do so.

## Sense of Humor

Joking, trick playing, and family "fooling around" play an important role in creative thinking. Family members often have comical names for one another and use a vocabulary understood only by them (Dacey 1989c). The parents and children in Dacey's study were asked to rate how much 13 traits, such as "having a high IQ" and "being popular with peers," contribute to creative thinking. "Sense of humor" was ranked in the top half by most of the responders.

Laughter is a response to incongruities or stories that disobey conventional expectations. Does that sound familiar? Stories that disobey conventional expectations are the essence of lateral thinking described earlier. Consider a one-liner like *If at first you don't succeed, skydiving may not be for you.* A joke like this may start out with part of a traditional saying *(If at first you don't succeed, try, try again)* and then surprise you. It disobeys conventional expectations and goes in an unexpected direction. Humor lights up several parts of the brain, starting with the thinking part that helps you understand the joke. To understand it, your mind must go in an unexpected direction, too. Consider, for example, that while other mathematicians and physicists were computing formulas, Einstein was imagining himself riding on a beam of light. That's a whole different approach—closer to the kind of thinking that makes humor possible than it is to analytical thinking.

Do you encourage humor in your classroom regularly? Or do you maintain a no-nonsense atmosphere? Students tend to model their behavior after what they see the teacher do. If you allow a certain degree of humor in your classroom, students see the value of humor and try to follow suit. Read to students from humorous books, such as *The Monster That Ate My Socks* by A. J. Cosmo (a great book for elementary students) or *Motel of the Mysteries* by David Macaulay (a great book for older students).

## Stimulus Flexibility

A stimulus is an object or action that makes us want to do something. It stimulates a reaction in us. Most objects and actions have this effect on us. It is the idea that tells us what an object is used for. For example, if you see an ice cream cone made of your favorite flavor, you will probably feel like eating it.

It is possible to have too rigid a sense of what an object must be used for. Creative people do not allow themselves to be so constricted. They may have a loaf of bread they want to cut in two, but they only have a string. They may loop the string around the middle of the loaf and pull on the ends. Voila! The job is done. Every successful inventor possesses flexibility regarding what objects are for or what actions can do.

People who have stimulus flexibility will tend to bend rules to fit their needs. They do not react to stimuli in conventional ways. If met with an ambiguous situation, a creative person does not assume that "normal" rules apply. People restricted by stimuli are often too focused on reactionary rules. And worse, when faced with ambiguity, they assume that rules are present when they really aren't. Imagine assigning students to draw something. Some of them will be quite uncomfortable until you specify what you want. Others will enjoy the freedom you have allowed them. The latter students are free from the fear of failure that often cripples the former. The fear of being wrong prevents students from reaching their creative potentials. Creative persons are not confined by limits set by others. They stretch their imaginations beyond their given guidelines, some being bold enough to forego the rules completely.

This is often seen when individuals are given the warm-up activity from Chapter One. In this test, an individual creates a story based on an ambiguous drawing. People often tell stories based on standards set by others. Because there is a picture of an animal next to a box, an average person, typically considered an individual not concerned with being creative, may tell a story about a theme that already exists. The average person's story options are narrowly based on what's offered in the drawing. Creative-minded people— those with a more developed creative ability—are able to think beyond the drawing and create a story that is not bound by the picture. Those individuals are able to imagine what exists beyond the stimuli. This allows them to use more imagination and creativity when creating ideas.

As explained earlier, functional freedom involves the capacity to see objects outside of their proper purpose. Most people cannot view an object beyond its defined use. Those who value creativity are more likely to free objects from their original task, giving them more imaginative license when solving problems. This is because creative people are able to imagine common items being used in uncommon ways.

The "Two-String Problem" at the beginning of Chapter Five is often used to measure stimulus flexibility. Many people cannot get beyond the usual function of the mousetrap to connect the two strings. Therefore, they are unable to find the solution to the test.

There are two recognized ways to foster stimulus flexibility. One way of fostering this flexibility is by thinking of many alternative solutions to problems. These solutions can be as simple as creating uses for ordinary objects or as complex as thinking of alternative sources of energy. Another way to foster stimulus flexibility is to think backward from a solution and to try to imagine how it originated. For instance, Leonardo da Vinci was the first to conceptualize the helicopter. And although he didn't build one, his design had the basic principles. We know that he began by drawing images of the anatomy of birds. From these drawings, he discerned elementary elements of flight. He then went on to translate them into a rough diagram that looks remarkably like a helicopter (da Vinci Inventions 2012). He called this idea an *aerial screw*.

How did he discover these principles? Even though students may lack the sophistication to retrace this thinking, their efforts to do so will foster the personality trait.

## Tolerance of Ambiguity

An ambiguous situation is one that has no guidelines to follow. Relevant facts are absent, rules are vague, and correct techniques are obscure. For many students, going to school for the first time is an ambiguous situation. What one student finds interesting may cause great tension in another. Being able to face ambiguity with an open mind is an important trait of the creative thinker. In fact, openness to new ideas in general is a main component of creativity.

Ambiguous situations exist on a continuum that extends from the very familiar to the very strange. Your best friend's face is very familiar, whereas a stranger with a badly scarred face and five missing front teeth would likely seem scary and very strange. Thus, emotional reactions to the environment extend on a continuum from boredom all the way to terror. The need for excitement and tolerance of the strange are key traits of the creative thinker. Figure 7.3 illustrates this continuum.

**Figure 7.3** The Ambiguity Continuum

| Situation: | Very Familiar | Somewhat Familiar | Somewhat Strange | Very Strange |
|---|---|---|---|---|

⟶

| Average Person: | Boredom | Interest | Excitement | Foreboding | Terror |
|---|---|---|---|---|---|
| Creative Person: | Boredom | Interest | Excitement | Foreboding | Terror |

The average person and the creative person start at the same location, but it takes a higher level of strangeness for the creative person to become frightened. Finding odd things thrilling rather than scary is useful for reacting creatively.

At Boston College, Dacey teaches "The Psychology of Creativity." Of the several evaluative criteria for the course, 25 percent is for a creative term project. "But what are the requirements for this project?," the students always ask. "There are none," he replies. "But you must give us some guidelines," the students complain. "No, I don't," is Dacey's answer. Students have complete freedom to do whatever they want! Total ambiguity. Students complain about the "unfairness" of the assignment, even though they voluntarily signed up for the elective course. In the end, all students usually agree it was the hardest term project they had ever been assigned, but many concur that it was also one from which they learned a great deal about creativity.

Tolerating ambiguity is not easy. It is, however, an essential idea that our students are to think creatively to solve the complex problems they will inevitably face. If the instructions for classroom problems are too explicit, students will get little practice confronting ambiguity. We urge that teachers slowly introduce uncertainty into their classes so that students can learn to handle it. This can be done, for example, by leaving out one of the parameters of a problem. Students must then attempt to discern what is missing from the instructions. This can be difficult for younger students, so introduce this slowly. A teacher can begin by omitting a step in the directions of how to make a peanut butter and jelly sandwich, for instance. Additionally, a teacher can also skip over two pages while reading a picture book and then have students try to figure out what happened on the skipped pages. This is excellent practice for situations they will later tackle in real life.

# Cultivating These Ten Traits in Students

If you are to take away anything from this chapter, know that you can and should foster the development of these 10 traits in your students. If you are successful, we guarantee that you will see an increase in their creative thinking abilities. Furthermore, students will have more interest in and retention of the content goals of the standards. How exactly can you cultivate these traits?

- **Model the traits whenever possible.** Stretch yourself to create imaginative ideas, and when you succeed, share your ideas, pointing out what you are doing. Explain to students how such thinking is different from logical thinking. Explain why such thinking is valued by society and therefore by you as the teacher.

- **Offer advice and explanations.** Be sure your students recognize and want to use the strategies exemplified in this book. Lecture if you must, but provide examples of the strategies to help students' understanding of the question at hand.

- **Be on the lookout for students who exhibit any of these 10 traits.** Praise and reinforce creative behavior so that other students see creativity as something positive.

- **Establish a center in the classroom where examples of the 10 traits are displayed.**

Cultivate these 10 traits in your students and watch them progress!

**Let's Think and Discuss**

1. What is one of the most challenging obstacles to overcome to allow for independent judgment in your classroom?

2. Describe an experience in which perseverance was a problem in your classroom. How did you handle it? Would you react differently in the future?

3. Have you ever been in a classroom where the teacher used humor? How can you use humor in your classroom to engage students?

# Chapter 8

# Fostering a Creative Classroom Atmosphere

## Creative Warm-Up

What appears in the middle of each month, occurs in every season except summer, and is in nighttime but never in daytime?

The classroom environment plays a very large role in students' creativity in school. Think about the atmosphere you need in order to be creative as a teacher (or anything else creative you do). Why does this environment work for you? What elements are in the space? Does it keep the distractions away? Do you deliberately place distractions to keep ideas fresh?

There are numerous stories of the lengths to which great creators have gone for motivation or inspiration. The German poet Friedrich Schiller, for example, kept rotten apples in his desk—he believed the smell inspired him. When that didn't work, he immersed his feet in ice-cold water! How is your furniture conducive to creativity? When we think of creative environments, we typically think of aesthetic elements. There is, however, much more to a creative atmosphere than just aesthetics. If students are to be creative, then create environments that enhance instead of hinder their creativity.

First, we need to examine the aesthetics of the classroom to set the stage so that all students produce to their maximum potential. Next, we will discuss how our assignments affect student creativity. We will also look at classroom management to see what options we have for grouping students and managing their creative work. And finally, we will consider the differences our relationships make to a creative atmosphere.

## Classroom Design

There are favorable physical conditions to enhance creative potential in students. The types of lessons and activities you plan should determine how the classroom is set up. Think about how the classroom space needs to function for the lesson or activity. For creativity, a multifunctional space is needed that is conducive to individual work, partner discussions, and group meetings. Desks should be moved at certain times, depending on the goal of the lesson. Flexibility is key for positive effects on learning (Amabile 1996).

When designing a classroom, there should be space for movement. Consider the traffic flow and plan accordingly. According to Clayton and Forton (2001), "Well designed traffic pathways can help students to move around the classroom safely, easily, and responsibly. This can improve transitions, help children to establish self-control, and generally support a productive and cooperative learning environment" (50). This also helps prevent disruptive behavior. Too little room for movement where students are bumping into each other and the furniture creates tension, conflict, and misbehavior in the classroom (2001). Prevent these problems by thoughtfully arranging desks and other furniture in your classroom.

To build a sense of community, creating group space is more important than creating individual space. According to Torrance (1995), "The classroom group may stimulate certain types of creative thinking. Children should learn early that creative ideas are shared and enjoyed by the group" (31). Whenever possible, have tables in your classroom. Tables are easily moved around and used for group meetings. Make sure that there are no places where students can hide; the teacher should be able to see the entire room from any angle. Limit the number of students allowed at the places designated for groups. This limits the tension and behavior problems caused by cramped spaces.

But some classrooms are small. To foster a sense of free flow, the teacher must create the illusion of a larger space. Nothing makes a space feel small like clutter. Put clutter inside cabinets or hide it under table skirts. Place collections neatly on shelves. Get rid of things you don't use or need. By doing these things, you will open up your space and make it feel larger. As mentioned previously, make sure furniture is moved out of walkways. If possible, use smaller pieces of furniture, such as benches, beanbags, or ottomans, to open the view across your classroom while providing seating choices at the same time. Large pieces of furniture should be placed against the wall. If given the choice, use a couple of large pieces of furniture instead of many small pieces of furniture, which can make the space feel cramped. Also, make sure your room is well lit. If you need to, bring in lamps and open up blinds to bring in more light. Color can also have a positive effect on how students feel about school. Pillows can be used to bring in a punch of color and can also soften the spaces. If you have the choice of wall paint, use soft tones of blues and greens to make it feel light and airy. Studies show that these calm colors optimize student creativity (Dudek 2000; Grangaard 1993).

Younger students need space to spread out on the floor. Area rugs that are positioned in strategic places in the room are perfect for this environment. Older students need more table space for small-group meetings. Naturally, classrooms that house older students contain more desks. Desks can be grouped in twos, fours, or sixes. Additionally, the horseshoe pattern provides opportunities for whole-group instruction as well as partner work. If space allows, bring in rugs, coffee tables, and comfortable seating. "Making furniture use-centered will enhance the overall experience. In the knowledge economy, where learning is not only continuous but also more informal and serendipitous, anything that makes the experience more positive will also increase learning" (Cornell 2002, 41).

Limit the number of items hung on the walls, but when decorating, make students' work part of the décor. This gives students a sense of pride and accomplishment. Work can be draped across one wall or even hung on cork strips and bulletin boards. Don't display too much at one time, and remember to rotate these displays often so that all students see their work. Use brightly colored informational posters to increase recall of important information. Research shows that students will recall up to 60 percent more when colored posters are used and will pay attention to the display up to 82 percent longer (Baird 2006). Select posters with care, being sure to use them sparingly as not to create clutter.

Select a theme or slogan for your room, such as insects, construction, smiley faces, sports, popular video game characters, superheroes, or movie stars. Stick with that theme when decorating. Begin with the classroom door and carry that theme into the space. This provides predictability and consistency and can help special needs students feel secure (Komendat 2010).

Because space will most likely be tight, there needs to be smart organization. Students need areas to place their personal items like lunches, bags, and supplies. If available, use cubbies or wall hangers. Organizers with compartments that drape over the backs of chairs work well for smaller supplies. When the classroom is organized, there will be more room for flexible meeting spaces.

Most teachers have a range of supplies for students to use in their classrooms. Many students respond well to color and need colorful tools to promote creative thinking. However, instead of simply providing traditional art supplies, provide unusual materials like empty thread spools, buttons, and scraps of material for student interaction. These unconventional tools are ideal for sparking divergent thinking. For example, Ryan Grenoble tells of Sun Jifa, a fisherman living in northern China, who lost both hands a few years ago during a fishing-related explosion (2012). Unable to afford prosthetics and desperately needing to work on his family farm, he took scrap metal and created his own prosthetic hands that are equipped with pulleys controlled by the movement of his elbows. Giving students the opportunity to explore with unconventional tools and materials also provides restrictions and limitations to encourage them to produce something original. And in the case of Sun Jifa, it can be helpful for real-life applications when needed.

# Assignments

To get the creative juices flowing, begin each day with a creative warm-up. Creative warm-ups can be posted on a bulletin board or poster outside your classroom to get other classes and parents involved. The answer to this chapter's creative warm-up is the letter "n." One year, I (Wendy) was put in charge of a bulletin board outside the hallway at the entrance to my school. I would post creative warm-up questions at the beginning of the school week to intrigue parents and students alike—and it worked! I had parents asking me if they had the right answer and students stopping me in the hallway to give their best guesses. I never knew the answer for sure until I looked it up to post on Friday morning. I wanted to be challenged to think creatively, too! Another way to get creative juices flowing is by decorating your classroom with unusual objects from the past and each week having students brainstorm ideas of what these objects could be used for today. These warm-ups provide opportunities for students to think laterally, which enhances their creativity.

There are many lateral thinking puzzles available online. Here are two examples:

There is a man who lives on the top floor of a very tall building. Every day, he takes the elevator down to the ground floor to leave the building to go to work. Upon returning from work, though, he can only travel halfway up in the elevator and has to walk the rest of the way unless it's raining! Why?

*(The man is very, very short and can only reach halfway up the buttons. However, if it is raining then he will have his umbrella with him and can press the higher buttons with it.)*

A man is wearing black—black shoes, socks, trousers, coat, gloves, and ski mask. He is walking down a back street with all the street lamps off. A black car is coming toward him with its lights off but somehow manages to stop in time. How did the driver see the man?

*(It was daytime.)*

Another way to keep creative minds engaged is by offering engaging choices within assignments. In her research, Denise de Souza Fleith (2000) found that teachers can encourage creativity by refraining from giving too many assignments and rules to students. Instead, teachers should give students choices and thus provide them opportunities to become aware of their creativity. These choices within assignments don't have to be vast. Just offer two or three choices to show what they learned. For example, allow students to write letters, create art, and/or perform a scene to show what they have learned. Figure 8.1 shows a variety of options for student assignments.

**Figure 8.1** Options to Encourage Creativity

| | | |
|---|---|---|
| • postcard | • letter | • diary |
| • bookmark | • recipe | • playlist |
| • bumper sticker | • puppet show | • bulletin board |
| • flip book | • talk show | • game |
| • cartoon | • press conference | • advertisement |
| • comic strip | • storyboard | • commercial |
| • song or rap | • animated short movie | • clay sculpture |
| • trading card | • how-to video | • photo essay |

It's important to put some thought into making these assignments so that students will truly be creative. For example, instead of assigning students to draw a book jacket, which they can just copy and adapt from their book, have them film a movie trailer to advertise the book. This will prove to be a great summarizing activity. What makes the video assignment more effective than the book jacket assignment is that students cannot copy something already out there. Instead, what they create will be truly original. Students can film movie trailers by drawing storyboard boxes on paper to show the scenes, videotaping puppets or stuffed animals reenacting the scenes, or having a full-blown cast of actors that includes their families and friends.

Providing open-ended assignments is important for creativity, but be sure to include some restrictions within those assignments. For example, don't assign projects by telling students that they can work on anything. Students need restrictions and parameters to force them to focus. For example, have students create something that demonstrates the theme "Wow!" It is up to the students to interpret "Wow!" creatively—an open-ended assignment. However, there should be choices: art, photography, writing, and video. The completed projects should be original and relate to the theme. If students opt to do a video, it should be limited to five minutes in length—these are the restrictions. Many of us might remember the popular television show *Extreme Makeover: Home Edition*. My (Wendy's) daughter decided to do a claymation video for her interpretation of "Wow!" based on this show. She didn't show the house being revealed. Instead, she showed a toy bus moving out of the way and a claymation person jumping up and down, doing somersaults, and crying a pool of water on the ground. Anyone who has watched the television show knows that half the fun is watching the reaction of the people when the house is revealed. It didn't matter that the house remained unseen; we knew that the house must have been amazing from the reaction of the claymation character. The open-ended instructions gave way to a truly creative project. Figure 8.2 shows the claymation character crying pools of water.

**Figure 8.2** Claymation Open-Ended Project

The key is giving students enough direction so that you don't get projects that are bottom of the barrel and completed in just five minutes. The following are some ideas for providing just enough direction for students:

- Specify the length of the project (e.g., 10–15 pages, 5 minutes, etc.)
- Assign a theme for students to work with (e.g., picture book about a tragedy)
- Help students with organization (e.g., storyboards, outlines, or checklists)

When teachers strike this balance while assigning open-ended projects, the sky is the limit and students' creativity can truly soar. An added benefit is that students show what they have learned, which gives you the assessment information you need.

Get creative ideas for assignments from things in real life. How many times have we sat in a movie theater, watching the previews before realizing that movie trailers would be a great book report assignment? A movie trailer can touch on all aspects of what makes a book interesting without giving away the ending. This idea applies to more than just language arts: students can use it to summarize historical events; music videos can explore science experiments and math solutions; or for geography class, students can come dressed as famous landmarks, such as Mount Rushmore, the pyramid of Giza, Rome's Coliseum, or the Taj Mahal, and give speeches as if the landmarks had feelings and could talk about their significance. The main idea is to adapt what we see in real life to create engaging and meaningful assignments that students can relate to while also allowing for creative interpretation.

# Classroom Management

Depending on the assignment and objective of each lesson, most creative work will be done individually. Other work will be done in groups, and some work will be a combination of the two. To be successful in today's world, students need practice doing all three.

As educators, it is our job to help students become independent, reliable workers, confident in their skills and willing to try new things. A certain amount of independence comes with age, but a teacher's encouragement and modeling of these skills can go a long way with students. Some students need more encouragement than others to build their confidence. There's a YouTube™ video—"Jessica's 'Daily Affirmation'"—that shows a three-year-old girl talking to herself in the bathroom mirror (2009). She lists all the things she likes about life, ranging from her school to her little sister to her hair. She tells herself that she can do anything great. In fact, she tells herself she can do anything better than anyone else and marches off to do it! After watching it, you can't help but feel that you need to stand in front of the mirror, list what you like about your life, and chant that you can do anything great—in fact, you can do it better than anyone else! At times, everyone needs encouragement to do the challenging tasks set before them. Simple reminders like these give students the confidence to independently try new things, take moderate risks, and do their best.

There are several creative tasks that are best done individually. One is the initial phase of brainstorming. Students will be less inhibited to write down their ideas within a certain time frame as compared to a group setting where their ideas may be judged. Later on, students may share their ideas with partners or in small groups. These ideas get combined and then evaluated. As students get older, brainstorming in groups can be more productive. With younger students, the teacher can lead the brainstorming sessions, being mindful to call on all students to give answers. (See more about brainstorming in Chapter Three.) Projects can also be created individually. While projects can be done in groups, the tricky part is dividing up the work fairly. For this reason, most teachers opt for individual projects. Checklists help students organize their work and stay on task whether the work is done at home or at school. The checklist in Figure 8.3 belongs to an assignment in which students write diaries from the perspectives of radishes and mealworms as a way to study decomposition. The checklist helps students make sure they have included everything in their projects.

**Figure 8.3** Diary Project Checklist

- ☐ Write from the perspective of the radish and the mealworm.
- ☐ Have drawings showing each stage.
- ☐ Include facts about each stage in a creative way, using the diary format.
- ☐ Each stage needs a new chapter in your diary.
- ☐ Include a table of contents.
- ☐ Give your diary a title and a cover page.

Working individually can be scary for some students. They often feel insecure about their work. To help with this, remind students that they *can* do the work with the hope of boosting their independent thinking. Remind them of past successes. Provide examples to guide them so that they know if they are on the right track. This can be done in simple ways like a message on the board saying, "You know you are on the right track when (give a clue)...." Keep a running list on the board of what to do when students feel stuck:

1. Take a deep breath and count to five.

2. Stand on your tippy toes ten times to get the blood flowing.

3. Review the task.

4. Try again.

5. If you are still stuck, raise your hand or ask a neighbor for help.

All these ideas promote healthy individual work. Using these types of techniques gives students the tools to be successful and build confidence in their work.

Working in groups can be tricky for teachers and students alike. Teachers worry about grading group work, helping students get along, and making sure students are on task. Too often, group work is unsuccessful, causing many teachers to shy away from assigning group work. But the lack of success could be due to the fact that we may have unrealistic expectations. Students are placed in groups and expected to not be distracted. Working with others will always be distracting to some degree. To get the best work out of our students, they should often select their own groups (Sarkisian 2012). Think about it—if you feel superior to others in your group or if you feel inferior to others in your group, then the group likely won't be productive. Either you will do all the work or do none of the work. It is important that students fully participate. If they feel comfortable working with certain people, then it is more likely that they will be productive. Some students may want to goof off no matter what, so setting the stage for productive group work is important. Let students know that if their group work is not productive, they will have to be assigned to groups and their contributions will be closely monitored. This helps students know the consequences if expectations are not met. Also, equally dividing the responsibilities helps group members stay on task, makes the project more meaningful, and gives teachers a way to assign individual grades. While this is not practical during a creative activity like group brainstorming, it does matter when working on group projects. See the Group Project Planner in Figure 8.4 to reference how students' work was divided up and how everyone was held accountable for the group project. The teacher assigned individual grades based on each student's contribution to the project.

**Figure 8.4** Group Project Planner

**Group Project Planner**

Group/Team Members: Kyle, Blake, Kris, Amber, Danielle.　　Project due date: 3/21/00

Project Title or Description: Colonial Pride　South

| Team Member | Task or Responsibility | Resources needed | Due date | Completed task |
|---|---|---|---|---|
| Blake _religion_ | Internet download image | Internet access + a computer | 3/19 | |
| Amber _economics_ | Digital camara Picture　Cover | Costumes + Digital Camara | 3/19 | |
| Danielle _social life_ | Overall page design | computer + P.P. | 3/19 | |
| Kris _Geography_ | Scanned picture | Computer, scanner + P.P. | 3/19 | |
| Kyle _government_ | Animation on Slide　Bibliography | computer + P.P. | 3/19 | |

A common mistake many teachers make is assuming that students should already understand how to work in groups. However, because of varied personalities and diverse academic abilities, the process is complex. In the book *Teamwork: What Must Go Right/What Can Go Wrong*, Larson and LaFasto say that there are stages that teams (groups) go through before functioning at their maximum capabilities (1989). It is helpful to know about these stages so that we don't become discouraged after our first few tries with group work. The stages are as follows:

**Stage 1—Forming:** As students first begin to meet together, they may be cautious. They often test the leadership of the group and try to find out what position they fill in the group.

Teachers can troubleshoot problems by using short icebreaker activities to help students get to know and trust one another.

**Stage 2—Storming:** This stage is typically the most difficult. Group members discuss and/or argue about the direction they should take and often feel outside their comfort zones.

The teacher should meet with groups as frequently as possible to check in on their progress. During this time, the teacher should serve as a moderator instead of trying to fix the problems for students.

**Stage 3—Norming:** Group members become more cooperative and concentrate on their work, thus making progress. Be sure to compliment them when you see groups working well.

**Stage 4—Performing:** The group knows the strengths and weaknesses of its members. They understand their roles in the group. Because of this, good ideas and quality products are produced.

For those students who have difficulty getting along with group members, you may need to model problem-solving situations. Have them role-play group situations to practice saying things the polite way. For example, it is better to say, "I have a problem with this plan" rather than "The plan you want to use is wrong." Come up with a signal that students can use to inform you that they need an intervention before things become worse. For instance, a concerned student could request help by showing two fingers pointed at the ceiling. Some teachers assume that middle school or high school students know how to work in groups, but more often than not, they don't. Many elementary school teachers don't give enough group work to make students competent at it. And there are a myriad of personalities to consider. Helping students navigate these group situations will benefit them later on in life as they encounter group settings in the future.

Without fail, it seems as if when we assign group work, the principal comes by the classroom and views what he or she believes to be chaos in action. When students are talking in their groups, it can be loud. Reminding students to keep their voices low can help with this. Some teachers worry—as we did—that their principals will not understand how this noise could be productive. Often, it only takes explaining to administrators what students are doing and pointing out how they are problem solving and sharing their thoughts. We find that explaining our goals—helping students become creative thinkers—gains support with our principals, especially if we invite them back to see the fruit of the students' labor.

Getting student buy-in is a key factor in getting groups to work. Naturally, students should be in charge of producing their specific guidelines for group work, but challenge them to suggest guidelines that omit the word *don't*, as in "Don't talk too loud." *Don't* invites students to challenge that rule. Instead, help students come to the conclusion that a cooperative classroom benefits and rewards *everyone*. Have students use this perspective when setting the guidelines for group work.

To change things up, it may be helpful to randomly assign students to groups or assign particular students to work together. The key is flexibility. Students need to change their groups every so often. Give these new groups time to see whether they work well together. This gives students the opportunity to work with others they would not have chosen and to value one another's differences. "Actively maintaining an atmosphere of respect for all social groups, religions, ethnicities and genders in the classroom is noted as being crucial to successful engagement with and of students and is a precursor to learning and creativity" (Banaji, Cranmer, and Perrotta 2000, 2).

To randomly group students effectively, use the technique called a "Q-sort." See Figure 8.5 for a visual. Here's how it works:

1. Write each student's name on a separate strip of paper.

2. Suppose you have twenty-one students in your class. Sort through the strips, selecting three students who most strongly demonstrate creative thinking in class. Put them in Pile 1.

3. From the remaining strips, choose three students who struggle with creative thinking. Put them in Pile 7.

4. From the remaining 15 strips, choose three students who demonstrate the most creative ability. Put them in Pile 2.

5. Select students using the same process for Pile 6 (least), Pile 3 (most), and Pile 5 (least). Put the last three slips in Pile 4.

6. Form five discussion groups of four students each (one group will have five members).

**Figure 8.5** Q-sort Grouping

| Group 1 | Two from Pile 1, Two from Pile 7<br><br>Write students' names in right column. | 1 _____<br>2 _____<br>3 _____<br>4 _____ |
|---------|------------------------------------------------------------------------------|----------------------------------------------------------------------------------|
| Group 2 | One from Pile 1, One from Pile 7, One from Pile 2, One from Pile 6 | 5 _____<br>6 _____<br>7 _____<br>8 _____ |
| Group 3 | Two from Pile 2, Two from Pile 6 | 9 _____<br>10 _____<br>11 _____<br>12 _____ |
| Group 4 | Two from Pile 3, Two from Pile 5 | 13 _____<br>14 _____<br>15 _____<br>16 _____ |
| Group 5 | One from Pile 3, One from Pile 5, Three from Pile 4 | 17 _____<br>18 _____<br>19 _____<br>20 _____ |

The Q-sort method makes grouping students more successful because with each pile you make, there are fewer students left in the pool to rate. It takes time, but groups tend to produce high-quality ideas, making the sorting process well worth the trouble.

## Relationships

The creative atmosphere hinges on the relationships formed with key individuals, such as administrators, teachers, parents, and students. How you use these relationships can determine the success of these strategies.

Administrators have a broader view of the school and its students, and most administrators care about producing creative thinkers. Make sure your superintendent, principal, and instructional specialists know that you care. If they don't know much about the importance of fostering creative thinking, request a meeting with them and lay out a plan. Begin with why your school needs to promote creativity (see Chapter One). Then, show them key strategies mentioned in this book, talking about how creativity and the standards can work together. Make your presentation professional and impressive. These individuals have access to funds that can buy materials and informative sources, such as *The Journal of Creative Behavior*, that can support your efforts. They may even know of grants and funding agencies that could be helpful to you. Also, administrators can organize meetings with teachers and parents to encourage creative growth in students. They can invite speakers, organize professional development, utilize their professional learning communities, and seek out webinars.

Within your school system and probably within your school, there are teachers who believe in creativity and the standards as you do. They are likely struggling with the same problems—especially time constraints. Consulting with these teachers will boost not only your morale but also your efficiency. Even if you teach different grade levels or content areas, you can share lesson ideas to cultivate creative thinking, usually with only a few minor modifications. Share lesson plans with colleagues, viewing what other teachers are doing in their classrooms to get good ideas. Visit one another's classrooms to see another teacher's creative instruction in action. The delight that teachers experience when they see others succeed is strong motivation.

You might also identify with other teachers regarding where you stand in the creative process. According to Shneiderman, there are three types of creative teachers: structuralists, inspirationalists, and situationalists (2007).

- As a *structuralist*, you may believe that people can be creative if they "follow an orderly method, typically described with several stages, such as preparation, incubation, illumination, and verification." (2007, 1).

- *Inspirationalists* advocate "working on unrelated problems, getting away to scenic locations, and viewing random photos or inkblots. Inspirationalists promote meditation, dreaming, and playful exploration. They seek to liberate thinking from old habits so as to break through to the 'aha!' moment of inspiration. This type advocates quickly exploring possibilities, concept mapping to discover unexpected relationships, and visualization to see the big picture" (2007, 1).

- The *situationalist* "recognizes that creative work is social. They seek to understand the motivation of creative people, their family history, and their personal relationships with challenging teachers, empathetic peers, or helpful mentors. They understand the need for distinctive forms of consultation at early stages when fear of rejection, ridicule, and rip-off are high … [T]he later stages are when validation, refinement, and dissemination are prominent. Situationalists seek to understand the motivating roles of rewards and recognition, as well as competition vs. collaboration" (2007, 2).

Think about which type of teacher you are, and then seek out one or both of the other two types within your circle of colleagues. These three types of thinkers benefit from working together. If a group of three teachers, each with a different viewpoint, discusses what can be done to increase creativity in their classrooms, excellent teaching strategies are more likely to result.

Based on countless interviews and parent-teacher conferences, we have learned that most parents want their kids trained in creative thinking. Many students' parents are likely to have jobs and experiences that call for imaginative thinking. Survey them for their ideas on projects that foster this skill, asking some to come to your classroom to offer tips and advice and even to volunteer in the classroom to support lessons and activities. You may be surprised at how many parents are willing and able to help you. One way to ensure parent support is by showing them how their child is progressing. Maintain a portfolio of each student's early efforts in becoming a creative thinker, and then demonstrate his or her progress at parent-teacher conferences. When parents see how your program is working, they will be more apt to provide you with valuable assistance.

Remember, an important part of teaching creative thinking is explaining to students why they need to think creatively. Once they have "bought in" to the idea, they can be valuable assets in producing lessons that meet both goals. Take, for example, the Remote Associates Test in which students have to think of a word that associates three disassociated words (a test explained in more detail in Chapter Nine). For example, what word associates *mouse*, *blue*, and *cottage*? The answer is *cheese*. When they understand this exercise, they can create examples that you can combine into a second exercise. We can assure you that students of various ages love to think of new words for this activity. This provides practice in thinking creatively as well as improving vocabulary. They will get even more creative practice by answering the second set of test questions. And they will have saved you the work of making up the second test! Students of all ages like to make up exercises for each other. They can also revise each other's work, make sure a partner understands an assignment, and encourage each other to reach greater levels of imagination and achievement. The better they get at creative thinking, the more helpful they can be to you in inventing new lessons. Finally, remember to help students feel that they can be freely creative. Students who are confident in themselves as learners will take risks and invest their time and attention to learn more content. They will tackle these risky tasks if they believe in their ultimate success (Caine and Caine 1991).

## Taking the First Steps

There is a lot of information to consider in this chapter. How does one begin to foster the most ideal creative atmosphere? As with any new thing, break down components into the following steps to ensure your success.

1. We believe the first consideration should be the physical classroom atmosphere. Make the changes that are within your ability. By making these changes first, the stage is set for students to be creative.

2. Next, commit yourself to working toward assigning more creative projects like the ones mentioned in this chapter. This gives students opportunities to stretch their creativity.

3. The types of assignments you design will naturally lead to how and if you need to group students. You don't want to group students without clear indications as to why you are grouping them. Let the assignments be your guide, and then work toward the most successful ways of grouping with your students.

4. Last but definitely not least, cultivate relationships throughout this process. Just being aware of forming the right kinds of relationships with administrators, teachers, parents, and students will help you to accomplish this goal.

**Let's Think and Discuss**

1. What is one idea adapted from the real world that you could use to engage students' creativity within assignments?

2. What adjustments will you make to your physical classroom to make it more conducive to creativity?

3. What key relationships do you first need to focus on in order to move forward with implementing creative thinking strategies in your classroom?

# Assessing Creativity

See if you can guess what these letters refer to:

a. 7 = D of the W

b. 26 = L of the A

c. 1,000 = AN

d. 200 = D for PG in M

e. 12 = S of the Z

Everyone loves the idea of using creative thinking strategies until it comes to assessment. How does one assess open-ended creative projects? Is it fair to compare student work to see which is the most creative and assign grades accordingly? What kinds of standards measure creative thinking? Should creative work even be assessed? Often it is these types of questions that keep us from including creative thinking strategies in our lessons. We do, however, believe there are solid answers to each of these questions when it comes to assessing creativity.

Imagine that all of the students in our classes will be assessed on their ability to dribble a basketball. Figure 9.1 could serve as a possible rubric.

**Figure 9.1** Basketball Rubric

| Ability | Letter Grade |
|---|---|
| The student can dribble with both hands. | A |
| The student can only dribble with one hand. | C |
| The student cannot dribble with either hand. | F |

It is one thing if students sign up for a basketball course as an elective, knowing full well that they will be graded on their growth in class and ability to play. It is another thing if students in our classes are assessed based on their ability—even if they have never had the opportunity to play or practice before—and are penalized accordingly. From experience, we know that some students are better equipped to play basketball well because they have practiced and developed their ability over time. We also know that physical education teachers typically grade students based on the effort put forth in class, not the ability. The ability to think creatively should be considered in the same way. Some students naturally think more creatively than others. This could be because of genetics or the fact that those students have had more opportunities and encouragement by family, friends, and former teachers to think this way.

As stated in earlier chapters, everyone has the capacity to be creative, and creative thinking is something that can improve. Developing one's creativity is work and takes both time and practice. The encouraging news? The sky is the limit to how much improvement can take place. No matter where we are on the creativity-thinking spectrum, there's *always* room for improvement.

As educators, we are not only responsible for producing students whose work meets important standards, but we are also responsible for preparing students to be creative thinkers for the real world. Since much of school is about grading students' mastery of specific grade-level standards, how students measure up to those standards is what ultimately matters to many. But creative thinking and how one applies those skills are what matter in the real world. It is a big task to think about how we can accomplish both of these tasks so that our students can enjoy the benefits of doing well in school and in life.

A teacher can help students become better creative thinkers by offering projects in which they can practice creative thinking. Because teachers need grades to show student progress, we must find ways to assess students' creative works so that grades can be assigned. While report cards don't measure creative thinking skills per se, we can still measure students' creative work using those important content standards. To do this fairly, assessments for creative projects must be as objective as possible, using measurable standards.

## Comparing Student Work

How do teachers assess creative products? In some classrooms, the project that appears to be most creative gets the highest grade and sets the bar for the rest of the class. There are a few problems with this practice.

Consider this example: A first-year teacher had her third-grade students design candy bars while reading *Charlie and the Chocolate Factory* by Roald Dahl. One student, Drew, created "Drewka's Chocolate Bar." Being a first-year teacher, she didn't think much of this until a more experienced colleague pointed out the creativeness of his project. Drew had his name as part of the brand for the chocolate bar. No one else in the class had done that, which made it unusual. Because the first-year teacher hadn't had the experience of seeing a variety of student projects at this point in her career, she didn't really know what she was looking for. She only knew that she wanted to give her students the opportunity to practice their creativity. It took an experienced educator to point out Drew's creativity and help the first-year teacher better define what creativity looked like in her classroom.

Some educators see many projects come across their desks and immediately know which ones seem to be unusual or extraordinary. However, regardless of your level of experience, creativity is very subjective, and what one teacher might consider creative, another teacher might dismiss as typical. And depending on a student's peers in a particular class, he or she might be the most creative or the least creative comparatively. A student should not be penalized by receiving a poor score on an assignment simply because he or she did not produce the most creative project.

We believe that if a student meets the content standard for the project, follows directions, and produces a quality project, then he or she should receive an A. For example, the assignment could be to create a puzzle that shows the concept of a food chain. The content standard is "understands how animals are related through a food chain." Students demonstrate their understanding of the content by creating puzzles. Students might create 3-D puzzles, puzzles with 100 pieces, or even puzzles with just four pieces that interlock. All of these student projects have followed the parameters of the assignment. But does the student with the 3-D puzzle receive the highest grade purely because it was the most creative project? Not necessarily. Students were asked to create puzzles that show their understanding of how animals are related through a food chain. If students created puzzles that show full mastery of the content standard and met the expectations for quality of work, they should receive an A whether the puzzle was 3-D or just four pieces.

## Crafting Rubrics

Well-crafted rubrics can aid teachers in assessing creative works. It takes careful thought when crafting rubrics to objectively grade creative works. To be objective, the criteria must be measurable and standards-based. Consider the following sample point-based rubric. Some of these points are objective, and others are not. Adjust the value of the points as appropriate.

- The student completed the project and followed directions. ___/5

- Two key vocabulary terms were included. ___/25

- Four facts were included. ___/25

- The finished project shows student understanding of the concept(s). ___/30

- The finished project shows student effort. ___/5

- The finished project is neat and legible. ___/5

- The project shows student creativity. ___/5

**The student completed the project and followed directions.** If the directions were followed and the project was completed, then that can be assessed objectively. A teacher can break apart these two components and assess them separately. Perhaps a student followed the directions but was unable to complete the project. Or perhaps a student completed the project but did not follow directions. Assign points to each criterion if needed, but the points should be minimal in comparison to the other points for the project.

**Two key vocabulary terms were included.** If the teacher asked for a certain number of vocabulary terms to be included, that can be assessed objectively. Most new concepts have at least a few key vocabulary terms. Making sure students use these terms correctly in context is often key to knowing if they grasp the concepts fully. If the project does not contain any written component where vocabulary can be used, then students can be assessed on vocabulary used during the verbal presentation or explanation of the project. Assign the points according to the importance of this criterion, such as five or ten points per term.

**Four facts were included.** Students can include key facts in their creative works. Consider the *Diary of a Strong Abolitionist* example from Chapter One. The student made sure to write a fictional piece from the perspective of a famous historical figure and include key facts in her writing. The student creatively demonstrated her knowledge that John Brown really did meet William Lloyd Garrison and they did not agree with each other. She quotes Garrison as saying that Brown was a disease to the abolitionists' cause. This fact was easily included in her creative writing. In the same way, a student could write about a visit to another planet in the solar system and include real facts within the work of fiction. Assign the points according to the importance of this criterion, such as five or ten points per fact.

**The finished project shows student understanding of the concept(s).** Perhaps the most important part to be assessed is this one. The goal of doing the project is that students learn the content. Assess the projects for evidence that students truly understood the concepts. Creative projects should never be busy work. Rather, they should be purposefully assigned as ways for students to apply and show what they have learned. For this reason, this criterion should be weighted more heavily than the others on the rubric.

**The finished project shows student effort.** This criterion is subjective unless the teacher observes students the entire time the project was being worked on. A teacher might think that the project showed little student effort, but was the teacher actually around to observe this when the student was working on the project? How can the teacher know for sure that the student put forth effort? Some students have to work incredibly hard for every grade that they receive. A teacher might give a student a poor score on this criterion only to have a parent contact them to say that their child spent the entire weekend working on the project plus extra hours after school the week before. Other students put forth very little effort and make perfect grades. They may have spent only an hour on the project total. Is it fair to grade students on their diverse ability to efficiently work on their projects?

**The finished project is neat and legible.** The teacher has to decide how important neatness is to the overall project. As far as handwriting is concerned, technology has changed our world so that today we mostly type out written work. Many school districts don't even offer handwriting instruction in the primary grades anymore. It is not a mystery why many students can no longer write neatly. For some students, neatness is a developmental issue. It should go without saying that the work should be legible. How can a teacher grade it if he or she cannot read it at all? On the other hand, projects like the food chain puzzle project need to be neat in the way the puzzle pieces fit together. Students might have included drawings of the food chain that to some degree should be identifiable. The teacher must consider how important neatness is to the project. Is neatness necessary to the quality of a project? Neatness, however, should never be used as a category just to fill in a rubric more fully. The criterion of neatness can be a subjective matter and should only be used when warranted.

**The project shows student creativity.** This criterion is commonly used in an attempt to measure creativity, something that is tough to assess objectively. We feel strongly that it is wrong to base an entire grade or the bulk of a grade on the creative aspect of the project because creativity is subjective to the audience. This doesn't necessarily mean that it can't be factored into the final grade. Creativity can be a small part of the grade, but the major overall grade should be based on standards that are objectively measureable. For this reason, few points should be assigned for this element of the project.

We feel that when it comes to assessing students' creative products, it is best to decide first on what you want to assess. Define the main goal of the project and then create criteria that objectively assess those goals. Even if a rubric is used, it might not be as clear as what is needed. Figure 9.2 is a rubric used to assess mathematical problem solving.

**Figure 9.2** Mathematical Problem-Solving Rubric

| Category | 4 | 3 | 2 | 1 |
|---|---|---|---|---|
| **Mathematical Reasoning** | Uses complex and refined mathematical reasoning | Uses effective mathematical reasoning | Shows some evidence of mathematical reasoning | Shows little evidence of mathematical reasoning |

On this rubric, there is a fine line between giving students a 4 or a 3. What separates *complex and refined* from *effective*? The criterion needs to be clear and concise, and you should communicate this to your students. Also consider Figure 9.3, a point-based rubric to assess a science project.

**Figure 9.3** Science Project Rubric

Provided an accurate, easy-to-follow diagram with labels to illustrate the procedure or the process being studied. Circle one of the following point values:

1  2  3  4  5  6  7  8  9  10

When determining the rating system for a rubric, it is typically best to have fewer choices than what is shown in Figure 9.3. Giving only a 0 = *Never*, 1 = *Sometimes*, 2 = *Usually*, and 3 = *Always* is better than using a ten-point system to choose from. It is tricky deciding what makes a 7 different from an 8 when assigning grades. This can be subjective, and it opens the door to grading students' work comparatively against their peers to decide whether a project merits a 7 or an 8, rather than measuring the final product against the standards of the project. The goal is to make these rubrics as objective and concise as possible.

It goes without saying that these assessments should be shared and discussed with students before they begin working on their projects. Students need to know the expectations so that they can attain the desired grades. For instance, students need to know to include factual information in their projects. They need a clear understanding of the expectations. An ideal rubric could have the following components:

| | | | |
|---|---|---|---|
| **Completeness and Directions** | **10 points**<br><br>The student completed the project and followed directions. | **5 points**<br><br>The student either completed the project or followed directions but did not do both. | **0 points**<br><br>The student did not complete the project or follow directions. |
| **Vocabulary** | **20 points**<br><br>Two key vocabulary terms were included. | **10 points**<br><br>Only one key vocabulary term was included. | **0 points**<br><br>No key vocabulary terms were included. |
| **Facts** | **20 points**<br><br>Two facts were included. | **10 points**<br><br>Only one fact was included. | **0 points**<br><br>No facts were included. |
| **Conceptual Understanding** | **50 points**<br><br>The finished project showed student understanding of the concept(s). | **30 points**<br><br>The finished project showed that the student only understood the concept(s) partially. | **0 points**<br><br>The finished project showed that the student did not grasp the concept(s) at all. |

Consider the following suggestions when creating your own rubrics.

1. First, think about what you want to measure. What is it that you want to accomplish by assigning this project?

2. Think of objective components for students to include in their projects that you can measure, such as vocabulary, facts, and completion.

3. Consider the point values as ranking the importance of these objective measures. If students fail to include one component, will they receive a failing grade? Find ways for students to redeem their projects, or allow them to fix the missing components for a better score.

# Encouraging Creative Growth

Often, a teacher assigns projects hoping to spark creativity in his or her students, only to find that students did not produce work to his or her expectations. This is not to say that you should throw the creative-thinking strategies found in this book out the window. In fact, that is exactly the opposite of what you should do. In order for students to improve their creative abilities, they must practice, and practice frequently. However, there are ways that you as the teacher can encourage students' creative growth by using the strategies in this book, ultimately supporting students in their efforts to become more creative individuals.

**Encourage students to take playful approaches to their projects.** Ask them to think about what would make this project fun to do. Should they use technology or connect the project to something in pop culture? Instead of having students create two-sided posters that just tell the differences between a coniferous forest and a deciduous forest, why not have them exercise creative dramatics and role-play as two animals that live in each forest to narrate the information from their points of view? This approach makes the work more engaging, and students will be creative in the process.

**Prompt creative ideas for projects by offering time for individual brainstorming.** Having done this, meet with students to discuss their unusual ideas, and offer other ideas if needed. This idea goes back to building relationships with your students. You have to know your students to know what makes them tick and what gets them excited to learn. For example, if the project is to create a picture book that tells about ordinal numbers, students might not be so excited to write this story. However, knowing that a particular student loves dogs could help spur him or her on to complete the project by simply mentioning that the student could tell the story from a dog's point of view. All of a sudden, the student is interested in writing this challenging story. In the end, students produce creative products while at the same time they grow in their creative-thinking ability. The product will be ultimately assessed according to how the student shows his or her understanding of ordinal numbers in a picture book format. Keep in mind that if a teacher shows students examples of projects, students typically copy these ideas because they want a good grade. This takes away from the open-endedness of the project, and as a result, it also takes away from the opportunity to develop and improve creative-thinking skills. The best way to get the creative juices flowing is by offering prompts that encourage open-ended creativity. See Figure 9.4 for sample prompts.

**Figure 9.4** Prompts for Getting the Creative Juices Flowing

- What could you do to make this project fun?
- How can you make this topic interesting and make others want to learn more?
- Have you ever thought about showing this from a different point of view?
- What about adding in some humor or jokes?
- What is the strangest or most unexpected way this could be shown?
- What could you do to surprise your audience?

The teacher is instrumental in helping students develop their creative-thinking skills. When a student turns in a project that is not as creative as you had hoped, make it a point to meet with that student one-on-one or in a small group to discuss ideas for the *next* project. Guide your students toward more creative products with these prompts. The goal is to develop and improve students' creative-thinking abilities.

While the first part of this chapter examined ways to grade creative products, the second part will show assessments that can be used to measure students' growth in creative thinking. The assessments in this second part test for more general creativity and are not specific to a content-area assignment. As previously noted, some of these assessments can be given as benchmarks throughout the year to assess student growth in creative-thinking skills. For example, a teacher can use the question, "How many ways can you use a stone?" at the beginning, middle, and end of the year to measure student growth. Answers should be evaluated for both fluency and originality. The more creative products students complete throughout the year, the more their creative-thinking skills will grow. Because creativity has to be practiced, these products help develop creative thinking in general.

## Assessments to Measure Creative Growth

We know how important it is to monitor the progress of our students whether in factual knowledge or in creative thinking. There is a complex array of methods for evaluating the latter. In this section, we provide examples for each category of measurement.

There are two central components to consider when choosing such a testing instrument. The first is *validity*. Validity is concerned with whether the test really measures what it is supposed to measure. How do scientists know? There are a number of ways. People known to be high in dogmatism (cult members, for example) should score low on a valid creativity test. If the opposite turns out to be true, it is likely that the creativity test is invalid. The second component to consider is *reliability*. Reliability has to do with whether the test evaluates that trait consistently. For instance, if those who score high on a test one day score low on it a month later—and no obvious experience has caused the change—the test is likely unreliable.

All of the creativity assessments we recommend possess these two components to an acceptable degree or higher. We give the source for each test (some are in the public domain and need no permission for their use) and examples taken from each.

It is common to assess complex abilities, like intelligence and creativity, by evaluating one of their basic elements. For example, we often measure IQ by testing for the ability to sort blocks into patterns. That activity is known to reflect one aspect of IQ (pattern recognition). As explained in Chapter One, this is also the case with creativity. Recall that the creative act typically occurs in two phases:

1.  Divergent thinking

2.  Convergent thinking

Divergent thinking begins the process of creative thinking as many different ideas are generated to explore a new situation or solve a problem. Intuition, which has access to the unconscious mind, prevails. This type of thinking usually can be described only in terms of its results, which are often quite imaginative. The thinker produces excellent outcomes, but can't explain why.

Convergent thinking occurs when each of the outcomes of divergent thinking is evaluated to see which idea is of the highest quality. This is achieved by comparing each of the outcomes to some standard of success. That is, how well does each of the divergently produced ideas meet the goal we set? It is a conscious process, and the steps it follows could be repeated by others. It is logical in that the thinker can recall the exact route he or she took to choose the best of the divergent ideas. The tests that follow are of aspects of divergent thinking (general, fluency, flexibility, originality, and elaboration). Although convergent thinking *is* the second half of every creative act, it is a matter of logical thinking.

Individuals with high levels of intelligence often demonstrate high levels of convergent thinking, but only creative thinkers are also good at divergent thinking. We will begin discussing creativity assessments by indicating some of the best examples of divergent thinking tests. You will notice that the test items may not necessarily be particularly creative. It is in the scoring methods that the validity of the test is evident. In many cases, we include instructions you would use if you decide to use the test.

You will also notice that most of the tests we recommend are copyrighted. We have permission to show exemplars of test questions but not scoring techniques. Therefore, in most cases, school systems will be required to purchase the test in order to obtain the scoring guide in its entirety.

Finally, we have said that all the measures we have described here are valid and reliable. Does this mean that they do an adequate job in today's evaluation-oriented world? Not necessarily. They are not targeted enough to assess creativity in the context of the new, more rigorous standards being established throughout the world today. They can tell you whether your students have improved their creative thinking in terms of elaboration, for example. However, none of them is specific to a subject-matter area.

But let us not forget the other purpose of teaching creative thinking: higher interest in achieving the skills and content knowledge of the standards. We are confident that you will see as good or better attainment of this objective as you have in the past. So don't be too concerned about not having standards-specific creativity tests. They are on the way.

## Measures of General Creative Ability

### Torrance® Test of Creative Thinking (TTCT)

The TTCT is a widely recognized measure of overall creative thinking (STS 2012).

**Directions:** Tell students to ask as many questions as they can about the image—questions that cannot be answered just by looking at it. A poor question would be, "Is the clown on his hands and knees?" You can see from the picture that he is. Students should ask questions as different from each other as they can. Don't just ask questions about the clown's clothes. Allow five minutes for students to think of as many questions as they can.

**Scoring:** Assess students based on each of Torrance's four criteria.

*Fluency*—one point for the total number of meaningful questions generated.

*Flexibility*—one point for the number of different categories of relevant responses.

Torrance found 21 categories, including the clown's clothing, his or her family and home, magical powers, characters not in the picture, what is beneath the surface of the water, etc.

*Originality*—one, two, or three points for how rare each response was in comparison to those made by other students.

*Elaboration*—one or more points for how much each question clearly goes beyond what the picture shows.

This test measures students' general creative abilities by having them transform *X*s into small drawings.

**Directions:** Give students large sheets of paper covered by orderly rows of *X*s. Have students make each *X* into a small drawing, each drawing different from the others (Panamericana 2012).

**Scoring:** Assess students based on each of Torrance's four criteria. As always with his criteria, scoring flexibility, originality, and elaboration are judgment calls. So as long as you strive for consistency in your scoring, you will be accurate enough.

*Fluency*—one point for the total number of *X*s that have drawings on them, no matter what the quality.

*Flexibility*—one point for the number of different categories drawn. In the sample, the table and T.V. would together earn one point (household items), and the skull and and alien would together earn one point (weird faces). All the rest fall into unique types (in our judgment).

*Originality*—one, two, or three points for how rare each response was in comparison to those made by other students. (Zero points if you've seen a similar drawing in most others' work; one point if by only 25% of students; two points if only by 10%; three points if unique.)

*Elaboration*—one or more points for how much each drawing clearly goes beyond the concept of an *X* (e.g., using the *X* to cross out something is a common use, not creative elaboration).

## Parental Evaluation of Children's Creativity (PECC)

The PECC test is one of several tests we will cite from rCAB© (2011), which stands for Runco Creativity Assessment Battery. rCAB© is a corporation led by Dr. Mark Runco, one of the leading researchers in creativity assessment in the world today. We have found the rCAB© tests to be both valid and reliable. This test asks parents to evaluate their own children.

**Directions:** Have parents complete the evaluation. Remind parents to be sure to (a) consider all seven possible answers, (b) take their time and carefully consider each item, and (c) remember that their ratings are completely confidential.

1. To what degree, or how often, is this child *artistic*?

| 1 | 2 | 3 | 4 | 5 | 6 | 7 |
|---|---|---|---|---|---|---|
| Rarely | Very little | Slightly | Moderately | Considerably | Very much | Extremely |

2. To what degree, or how often, is this child *adventurous*?

| 1 | 2 | 3 | 4 | 5 | 6 | 7 |
|---|---|---|---|---|---|---|
| Rarely | Very little | Slightly | Moderately | Considerably | Very much | Extremely |

**Scoring:** The higher the score, the higher the student's ability as creative thinker is likely to be.

## Teacher's Evaluation of Students' Creativity (TESC)

This test is very similar to PECC, but teachers do the evaluating instead (rCAB© 2011).

**Directions:** Complete one evaluation for each of your students who are participating. Be sure to (a) consider all seven possible answers, (b) take your time and carefully consider each item, and (c) remember that your ratings are completely confidential.

**1.** To what degree, or how often, is this child *self-directed*?

| 1 | 2 | 3 | 4 | 5 | 6 | 7 |
|---|---|---|---|---|---|---|
| Rarely | Very little | Slightly | Moderately | Considerably | Very much | Extremely |

**2.** To what degree, or how often, is this child *curious*?

| 1 | 2 | 3 | 4 | 5 | 6 | 7 |
|---|---|---|---|---|---|---|
| Rarely | Very little | Slightly | Moderately | Considerably | Very much | Extremely |

**Scoring:** The higher the score, the higher the student's ability as creative thinker is likely to be.

# Fluency Tests

Fluency is a type of divergent thinking. It refers to the ability to generate lots of ideas. Remember, people who are gifted in this trait don't always have high-quality ideas. They're good at quantity of output. The best of them are also extraordinary judges of the quality of their concepts, but for fluency, we are only looking at quantity.

## The Titles Game

The Titles Game test (rCAB© 2011) asks students to think of lots of ideas for each kind of title.

**Directions:** Have students list alternative titles for the movies, plays, and books. Remind them that spelling does not matter, there are no grades for this, and to have fun as they list as many alternatives as they can.

**1.** List alternative titles for the movie *Titanic*.

**2.** List alternative titles for the play *Romeo and Juliet*.

**3.** List alternative titles for *The Cat in the Hat* by Dr. Seuss.

**Scoring:** The higher the score (i.e., the more titles listed), the higher the student's ability as a creative thinker is likely to be.

## CP Frequency

The CP Frequency test measures students' fluency. In this test, students generate lists of possible uses of an ambiguous figure.

**Directions:** Have students look at the figure, thinking about what they see and what it might be. Then, have students list as many things as they can, even if they think their ideas are not very good. Remind them to think of this as a game and have fun with it! The more ideas they list, the better.

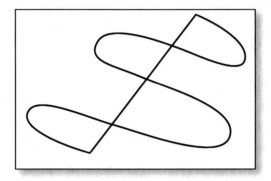

**Scoring:** The higher the score (i.e., the more ideas listed), the higher the student's ability as a creative thinker is likely to be.

## The SWOT Test

The SWOT Test is based on the "SWOT" concept from stock investing: Strengths, Weaknesses, Opportunities, and Threats (Investopedia 2010). This test measures these four aspects from the standpoint of creative thinking (rCAB© 2011).

**Directions:** Have students answer the questions that follow. Remind them that there are no wrong answers. What matters is that they are providing as many ideas as they can for each question. Remind them to think about possibilities and hypothetical ideas drawn from their experiences.

1. What are the *strengths* of this class?

2. What *opportunities* can or should this class explore?

**Scoring:** The higher the score (i.e., the more ideas listed), the higher the student's ability as a creative thinker is likely to be.

## Realistic Problems Test

The Realistic Problems Test involves real difficulties in students' lives and ideas for resolving them (rCAB© 2011).

**Directions:** Have students answer the questions.

**Question 1a**—List three problems you have been having lately with your siblings, friends, or classmates (any individual your age). For instance, you might have noticed that one of them has been ignoring you. These problems might be real, or they might be imaginary. Do not limit yourself. The more problems you can list, the better.

**Question 1b**—Go back and select one of the problems you listed. Next, list possible solutions to that problem. Use your imagination and be original! The more solutions you list, the better. (Do not list new problems—be certain you are listing solutions or actions that help resolve the problem.)

**Scoring:** The higher the score (i.e., the more solutions listed), the higher the student's ability as a creative thinker is likely to be.

# Flexibility Tests

Flexibility tests emphasize the thinker's ability to generate ideas about a single concept, ideas that vary significantly from one another. Variety is the goal here as opposed to quantity that fluency emphasizes. The more it characterizes a student's thinking, the more creativity is likely to result.

## What Do the Letters Stand For?

IQ tests usually measure verbal and mathematical skills. There are "correct" answers to this test, but credit is given for alternative responses that are right. The purpose of the instrument is to measure students' "associative flexibility"

(Enchanted Mind 2012). In other words, how fluid are their thoughts? Are they good at detecting obscure associations between ideas?

**Directions:** Tell students that each problem contains the initial letters of the words that will make a phrase. Have them guess what the letters refer to. There may be more than one answer to some of the questions."

**a.** 7 = D of the W

**b.** 26 = L of the A

**c.** 1,000 = AN

**d.** 200 = D for PG in M

**e.** 12 = S of the Z

**Scoring:** The answer key for this test, which also served as the creative warm-up at the beginning of the chapter, is as follows:

**a.** 7 = Days of the Week

**b.** 26 = Letters of the Alphabet

**c.** 1,000 = Arabian Nights

**d.** 200 = Dollars for Passing Go in Monopoly™

**e.** 12 = Signs of the Zodiac

## Students' Idea Preferences

This game asks students to tell how much they like certain ideas (rCAB© 2011). They will be asked to choose between Student A's ideas and Student B's ideas. One student demonstrates flexibility and the other does not.

**Directions:** Read the statements that follow. For each statement, whose ideas do you like better? Circle either Student A or Student B to tell whose ideas you liked best.

1. Students A and B were asked to "make a list of round things."
   Student A said "basketball, volleyball, softball, tetherball, golf ball."
   Student B said "basketball, the moon, a pumpkin, eyeball, zero."

2. Students A and Student B were asked to "make a list things on wheels."
   Student A said "car, truck, motorcycle, bike, skateboard."
   Student B said "car, police, groceries, Wile E. Coyote, unicycles."

**Scoring:** For each pairing, Student B's responses indicate more flexibility (i.e., the answers are more varied from each other). The total number of choices of flexible answers shows level of creative-thinking ability.

## Funnel Test

The Funnel Test measures students' flexibility. In this test, students generate lists of as many varied uses for an ambiguous figure as possible.

**Directions:** Have students look at the figure, thinking about what they see. Tell them to list as many different things as they can that this figure might be. Remind them to think of this as a game and have fun with it! The more different ideas they have, the higher their score will be.

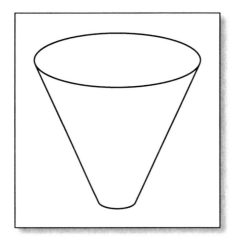

**Scoring:** The higher the score for "really different things" (i.e., the more varied ideas listed), the higher the student's ability as a creative thinker is likely to be.

## Originality Tests

As you know by now, our criterion of originality is that it differs significantly from products of others.

### Activity Check List

Also an rCAB© (2011) test, the Activity Check List is an inventory, not a test. The inventory is a list of activities and accomplishments in various fields of study.

**Directions:** Instruct students to circle the response that best describes how often they do the activity. Remind them to answer each question. These should be activities they do outside of school.

1. How many times have you written poetry?

   Never          Once or twice          3–5 times          More than 5 times

2. How many times have you helped build a structure that you designed?

   Never          Once or twice          3–5 times          More than 5 times

**Scoring:** The higher the frequency of these activities, the higher the student's ability as a creative thinker is likely to be.

### RIBS-D

People have ideas all the time (rCAB© 2011). They may not always act on them or talk about them, but ideas are a common part of our thinking. This survey asks about your ideas and how frequently you have certain kinds of ideas.

**Directions:** Have students read each item carefully, and then circle the answer that shows how often they have that type of idea. Remind them to answer honestly, not how they think they should.

1. How often have you had ideas about how to make something work better?

   Never      1–2 times         Once each        Several times        Daily
              per year          month            each week

2. How often have you had ideas about using the scientific method to understand a problem in your day-to-day life?

   Never      1–2 times         Once each        Several times        Daily
              per year          month            each week

**Scoring:** The higher the frequency of these ideas, the higher the student's ability as a creative thinker is likely to be.

## The Nine-Dot Exercise

This exercise measures the ability to think in unorthodox ways. Students will need to use their imaginations to reach a solution.

**Directions:** Instruct students to draw exactly four straight lines that go through all nine dots without lifting the pencil from the paper, but only through each dot once. This means that each of the four lines is connected to the line before it. Explain that they can use the first set of dots to practice and the second set to show their final answer.

*Hint:* If you still can't get it after you have tried two different ways, ask if there are any limitations you have assumed in trying to solve this problem.

**Scoring:** Starting in the upper left-hand corner, draw a line through the lower left-hand corner, long enough so that a second line drawn from it intersects two dots and ends at the level of the top row of dots. Continue the third segment of the line back to the top-left corner, and then extend the fourth part of the line diagonally through the two remaining dots. Students who get the correct answer within five minutes are likely to be more capable of original thinking than those who don't.

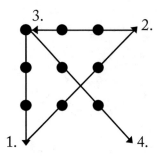

### The Two-String Test

The Two-String Test measures students' originality by asking them to creatively resolve a problem situation.

**Directions:** Instruct students to find a way for the boy to tie the two strings together. Explain that the two strings are too far apart to reach at the same time. Somehow, the boys needs to get hold of one of the strings while holding the other so that he can tie them together. There is one item available for finding the solution—a wooden mousetrap. Mousetraps are only about four inches long, so they are not long enough to use to reach the second string, no matter how tall he is. When students think of how the boy can tie the strings together, have them write their solutions on a separate sheet of paper.

**Scoring:** Student should mention attaching the mousetrap to one of the strings and then swinging it away from them. Then, they could grasp the other string, catching the first string as the mousetrap swings back. Then, the two strings may be tied together. Students who get the correct answer within five minutes are likely to be more capable of original thinking than those who don't.

*Note:* This is the kind of test that could be scored electronically using a computer. To do this, have students type their answers in a word processing program. Then, conduct a search for key words in students' responses. The computer searches through the responses for the key word (e.g., *swing*). We find that if the key word is there, the student's solution is correct. If not, then it's not.

## The Remote Associates Test

The Remote Associates Test was designed to measure the ability to flexibly and freely associate ideas (Mednick and Mednick 1967). The student is given three words and asked to find a fourth word that is related to the other three. The first three words may seem to have little or no similarity to each other. But all three are associated with the fourth word. For example, what word is related to these three words?

cookies     sixteen     heart

The answer is *sweet*. Cookies are sweet. *Sweet* is part of the phrase *sweet sixteen*. It is also part of the word *sweetheart*.

What word is related to these three words?

poke     go     molasses

The answer is *slow*. *Slow* goes with each of the other words: *slow poke*, *go slow*, *slow as molasses*. The fourth word may be related to the other three for various reasons. The difficulty of this test can be adjusted by making one of the matched words one that is less closely related to the answer.

**Directions:** Have students write the word they think is correct in the space to the right of each set of words.

1. flap   tire   beanstalk     _____

2. mountain   up   sky     _____

3. package   cardboard   send     _____

4. surprise   group   birthday     _____

5. madman   acorn   pecan     _____

6. plug   high   electric     _____

7. butterfly   catch   fish     _____

**8.** flash    bulb    heavy    _____

**9.** slit    knife    bandage    _____

**10.** snow    color    black    _____

**11.** out    home    jail    _____

**12.** slugger    wood    ball    _____

**13.** stage    game    actor    _____

**14.** Roman    arithmetic    VII    _____

**15.** cat    white    dark    _____

**16.** round    snow    beach    _____

**17.** bark    Eskimo    ocean    _____

**18.** bell    rings    aisle    _____

**Scoring:** Use the following answer key to assess students' answers. The higher the score (i.e., the more questions correctly answered), the higher the student's ability as a creative thinker is likely to be.

| | | |
|---|---|---|
| **1.** jack | **7.** net | **13.** play |
| **2.** grade, high | **8.** light | **14.** numeral |
| **3.** box | **9.** cut | **15.** black |
| **4.** party | **10.** white | **16.** ball |
| **5.** nut | **11.** house | **17.** seal |
| **6.** wire | **12.** bat | **18.** wedding |

# Elaboration Tests

Elaboration is the hardest of the four abilities to measure because its presence is something of a judgment call. Nevertheless, experts agree that you can usually tell it when you see it. Take, for example, the second grader's suggestion that kids' books would be more fun if they contained several of those mechanisms that play music when you open a greeting card. There are tests that attempt to assess elaboration indirectly but more objectively. The following tests are two examples:

## "Impossible" Tests

For these tests, students are asked questions for which there is no correct, objective answer. Those who enjoy wrestling with such "mind-breakers," situations in which logical parameters do not exist, are more likely to be creative. People low in creativity are likely to give up immediately.

**Directions:** Have students provide answers to the following questions.

1. How could you measure the speed of a bullet with no scientific instruments?

2. How could you measure the beauty of a face?

3. How could you teach a monkey to read a book?

4. How could you measure the distance from our planet to the edge of the universe without scientific instruments?

**Scoring:** Measure success by the time spent coming up with answers. The longer people struggle with these questions, the higher their score on other creativity tests and evaluations of problem-solving ability (FairTest 2012).

## The Welsh Figure Preference Test (WFPT)

The WFPT (Welsh 2012) consists of 400 black and white figures arranged on a neutral gray background in a booklet of eight figures per page. The figures were drawn to generate a wide variety of objects from simple geometric forms to complex, diverse patterns and designs. They were drawn with many variations to include differences in line quality, shape, content, and other aspects of the figure. Of course, in the actual tests, the more disordered, asymmetrical of the two paired pictures will sometimes be first and sometimes second.

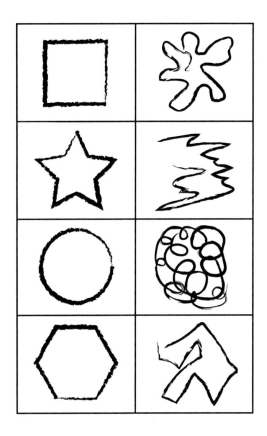

**Directions:** Have students decide which figure they prefer for each horizontal pair.

**Scoring:** The more disordered, asymmetrical pairs students choose, the higher their abilities as creative thinkers are likely to be.

## In Summary

Creative-thinking strategies have many benefits both in school and in the real world. These strategies make standards-based content more engaging and meaningful for students. Because of this, students are motivated to learn and will retain the information better. The strategies also prepare students for the workplace where they will likely need to collaborate with creative ideas and solutions.

Some tests measure students' content knowledge through their creative projects, activities, etc. Others purely measure students' creative thinking. In combination, these assessments can provide teachers with valuable information to help support their students' creativity throughout the school year.

 ## Let's Think and Discuss

1. Which of these tests would be helpful in assessing your students and why?

2. When would you use any of these tests in your classroom?

3. How can these tests benefit both you and your students?

# Chapter 10

# Nurturing Your Own Creative Spirit

## Creative Warm-Up

If you could be anyone, who would you be, and why?

"When we live more creatively, boredom is banished and every moment holds the promise of a fresh discovery" (Csikszentmihalyi 1996, 344).

As educators, being creative in something is not a luxury. Rather, it is the key to improving the quality of our lives. Every day is filled with opportunities for problem solving and innovation. But we are faced with challenges that make creative instruction difficult to implement. All of our students must meet grade-level standards even though they come through our doors at different academic levels. Our lessons need to be engaging so that students will learn. Our colleagues can be difficult to work with at times. Instead of dreading these challenging situations, we can utilize them as opportunities to fill our days with the wonder and excitement that comes from creativity. We discover better ideas for teaching a difficult concept so that our students can grasp it more easily. Our improved lessons will engage more students. We will figure out new ways to inspire the teachers around us so that they will join us on this journey of creative discovery. Most importantly, our work will be rewarding because we know we are making a difference.

There are countless suggestions for ways to nurture your creative spirit. We have selected a few to discuss in this final chapter. Through our experiences, the ones that have made the biggest difference in our creativity include being lifelong learners, developing diverse networks, committing to the work of creativity, and relaxing and resting.

## Be a Lifelong Learner

Life is busy, and our work takes up much of our time. In some cases, single parents hold two jobs to make ends meet. This doesn't leave much time for creative activity. There are real limitations to how much a person can do. But for most of us, it is only a matter of mental focus.

If you have never pursued a goal outside your work or family, then begin by asking yourself these questions:

- What are the things (outside of work and family) that interest me?

- What would I like to learn about?

- What have I always wanted to do but haven't made the time to learn how to do?

Is your answer scrapbooking, kayaking, playing the violin, weightlifting, refurbishing furniture, developing apps, painting, or knitting? Your answer to the creative warm-up at the beginning of this chapter may provide some clues as to what you would like to do. What kinds of things do these individuals do that you admire? Start with one thing you want to learn. Try it out. If you find you don't like it, then try something else. If you find that you do enjoy it, then pursue it further. To a certain degree, most skills can be learned. Some interests require that we take a class or read literature. There are countless how-to videos online that show step-by-step directions for learning a skill, and some communities even offer free courses. For example, the Massachusetts Institute of Technology (MIT) and other colleges have put most of their courses online, and they can be taken for free. Take the necessary steps to seek out these opportunities to expand your knowledge.

Next, ask this question: *What is an attainable goal I can set for myself?* For example, you don't want to set the goal of running in a marathon if you have never walked around the block. Instead, a more attainable goal would be to run a 5K race. That goal will certainly stretch you to learn how to run, but it won't defeat you before you begin. Your goals can grow as you attain them. If you find that completing a 5K race is exhilarating (and we bet you will), then set a goal for a half marathon next.

It can be scary to take the steps necessary to follow our goals, but taking moderate risks is what makes us feel alive. Taking risks is satisfying when we achieve something that, at first, we deemed too difficult to do. Write down these goals, and keep them in a safe place so that you can look at them from time to time. Tell those closest to you about these goals so that they can provide positive encouragement and support on the days you feel unmotivated or want to give up.

In addition to these goals, plan small risks that can be attained on a daily basis. For example, commit to doing something unpredictable each day like talking to a stranger, voicing an unpopular opinion, changing your hairstyle, or going somewhere new. Comfortable routines can restrict and limit the future (Csikszentmihalyi 1996). So break out of your comfort zone and do something unexpected. You will be surprised at what these little changes can do for you.

Why do some people devote their time to things that are not necessarily rewarded with fame or money like rock climbing, dancing, chess, or music? These experiences are what Csikszentmihalyi calls "painful, risky, and difficult activities that stretch the person's capacity and involve an element of novelty and discovery" (1996, 110). People who performed these tasks in Csikszentmihalyi's studies were intrinsically motivated to do these tasks and experienced an automatic, effortless, and highly focused state of consciousness. This highly focused state of consciousness is what we call *flow*. Flow can be defined as the state of mind or state of experience that we feel when we are totally involved in what we are doing. Flow can happen when we engage in a difficult yet possible task. If a task is too difficult, we feel stressed. On the other hand, if a task is easy, we become bored. The key is to involve ourselves in tasks that provide the right amount of challenge. During flow, we lose all sense of time. For example, have you ever been working on something, thinking that perhaps 30 minutes has passed, and then you realize when you look at the clock that it has been an hour and a half? You were so engrossed in the task that time stood still. The challenge of the task was perfect for you because even though it was difficult, you had the skills to be successful in it. In those moments, you experienced flow. Csikszentmihalyi advocates that flow is the key to happiness. To experience flow, we must take on challenges in our everyday lives.

We must continue to challenge ourselves in our jobs, too. Establish teaching challenges for yourself. Brainstorm ideas and then make a plan for how to teach a lesson differently from the way you did it last year. Decide how you will improve communication with parents at student conferences. Think of tangible things you can do to develop camaraderie among your fellow teachers like planning a happy hour every so often.

Being lifelong learners has many other benefits. By having so many diverse experiences, you will be more attractive and interesting to others. Learning something new boosts your self-esteem because you have achieved something that you thought was hard. Learning also enhances your mental fitness, which matters immensely as you age. Stretching your mind to learn new things improves your cognition and perception (Doidge 2007). If you don't use it, you will lose it.

## Develop Diverse Networks

There are times when we will need to collaborate with others so that we can brainstorm and bounce ideas around. For this very reason, it is important to have groups of diverse friends. Having a diverse network of people to go to can unexpectedly bring about new ideas. For example, a friend in a different field of expertise will naturally provide a new way of looking at a situation. Ideas from others in different fields can help us find the solutions we need. It can also help us to better understand situations. Purposefully seek out unique people to befriend. It won't be difficult to connect with others who, like you, set goals and seek to achieve them.

Not only do we need to surround ourselves with diverse people, but we also need diverse experiences. For example, you might visit a museum you've never been to before. This diversity will help us connect the dots between things that, at first glance, seem very different. People without diverse know-how won't be able to connect ideas because they lack the experiences to draw from. Having a broader field naturally gives us unique ideas. This idea goes hand in hand with trying new things, such as running a half marathon, traveling to a new destination, meeting new people, or honing a new skill.

## Commit to the Work of Creativity

Over the past years, I (Wendy) have taught myself to reupholster furniture. This all began because I couldn't afford to pay someone to do it. Now, I enjoy the challenge. It is like a puzzle that I take apart and figure out how to put back together. A while back, I purchased an antique settee. It sat there for a few weeks, and I found myself getting frustrated that I didn't have the complete plan in my mind. What fabric will I use? What colors will I paint it? Where should it go? My mind scolded me: *A good designer would know the plan right away!* But that's not really true, and I learned a lesson about creativity through this. As I described some of my ideas to a friend, I realized that creativity is a journey. The plan will unfold as I commit myself to work on it. I might make a few mistakes like selecting the wrong fabric. I might learn that a big print looks better than a small print. I'll have to correct these mistakes. The first paint I apply might not look right, so I'll repaint it. Creativity is a learning process spurred by hard work. Once it is done right, I'll feel satisfied and proud of it.

We cannot be creative in something if we don't take the time to develop the skills for it. We must commit to working toward the goal. For example, just *wanting* to be a guitar player does us no good if we don't *learn* how to play. It takes years to cultivate the skills to play the guitar well enough to perform for others in a coffeehouse. If that is the goal, then we must first learn to play the guitar and then faithfully practice so that we become better at it. Only then can we hope to someday play well enough to perform and compose some of our own songs.

Creativity requires focus and discipline. To be good at something, commit to the necessary work. That means that we must put in the time necessary to hone our skills. Olympians don't just get out there and compete. They work for years at their skill. The daily hours are long and strenuous. They deny themselves junk food and desserts. All of this is for that one moment of glory that we watch on television. Sometimes the work required to be creative is not fun. This is where discipline plays a large role in our creativity. Push through the difficult times and stay committed. In the end, the payoff will be worth the trouble.

## Relaxing and Resting

In order to be the best teachers we can be, it is imperative that we take time to relax and rest. Highly creative people typically need more rest to be at their best (Csikszentmihalyi 1996). The only way to continue to be fresh and enthusiastic in our work is by getting the rest that we need. If necessary and possible, take those vacation days and recharge so that you can be the best teacher, daughter, son, parent, or spouse you can be. Surround yourself with things you love and people who love you. Take time to smell the roses. Make it a daily point to notice one unusual thing around you. Keep a gratitude journal. All these tips will keep you refreshed.

Another key to relaxing is knowing when to walk away so that a problem can incubate for a while. Sometimes, we might focus on the wrong solution to a problem. Only when we relax can the right solution come to mind. This can happen when we physically walk away. It can be a simple act of getting up and moving rooms or walking your dog. Good ideas tend to come when we are not focused on the problem at hand. Legend has it that Leonardo da Vinci said, "You should often amuse yourself when you take a walk for recreation, in watching and taking note of the attitudes and actions of men as they talk and dispute, or laugh or come to blows with one another…noting these down with rapid strokes, in a little pocket-book which you ought always to carry with you" (The Painter's Keys 2012).

Have you noticed that good ideas often come while driving or in the shower? Our brains are free to wander and explore during these times. Unconsciously, the brain is searching for the right answer. When the right answer hits us, it feels like an unexpected blessing, and right away we know that it is the answer we've been looking for.

In conclusion, we hope this book will measurably foster the creative-thinking skills of you and your students. We know that there are countless books on creativity, but our goal is to inform you as an educator about the key components you need to know so that you can support creativity in your classroom. Understanding how creative thinking works will make you more aware of ways to implement strategies. The strategies that promote fluency, flexibility, originality, and elaboration will give students a well-rounded set of tools to control, guide, and develop their creative thinking. Understanding the traits of creative students will help you identify and encourage these traits in your students. Knowing how to create an atmosphere that is conducive to creative thinking will make all the difference in your classroom. And finally, don't forget to nurture your own personal creativity. After all, you are the key!

 ## Let's Think and Discuss

1. What are some goals that you would like to achieve, and how can you make a plan for achieving them?

2. What daily risks will you take to nurture your own creativity?

3. What are some ways you will seek to be more creative in your job as an educator?

# References Cited

Amabile, Teresa M. 1996. *Creativity in Context: Update to the Social Psychology of Creativity*. Boulder, CO: Westview Press.

Ask the Inventors. 2012. "The Great Idea." http://www.asktheinventors .com/faq.html#top.

Baird, David. 2006. "A Splash of Color, a Dash of Learning." *The Journal* 33 (6): 38.

Banaji, Shakuntala, Sue Cranmer, and Carlo Perrotta. 2000. "Expert Perspectives on Creativity and Innovation in European Schools and Teacher Training." Edited by Anusca Ferrari, Romina Cahcia, and Yves Punie. Accessed October 4, 2012. http://eprints.lse.ac.uk.30042.

Barron, Frank. 1988. "Putting Creativity to Work." In *The Nature of Creativity*, edited by R. J. Stenberg, 76–98. New York: Cambridge University Press.

Barry, Anne Marie. 1997. *Visual Intelligence: Perception, Image, and Manipulation in Visual Communication*. New York: University Press.

Bedingfield, Natasha. 2010. "Can't Fall Down." Song from *Strip Me*, compact disc. Phonogenic Records. Co-written by Natasha Bedingfield, Steve Kniper, Andrew Frampton, and Wayne Wilkins.

Bishop, Christopher. 2006. *Pattern Recognition and Machine Learning*. Berlin: Springer.

Block, Cathy. 1997. *Teaching the Language Arts: Expanding Thinking through Student-Centered Instruction*. Needham, MA: Allyn & Bacon.

Bloom, Benjamin, and David Krathwohl. 1956. *Taxonomy of Educational Objectives: The Classification of Educational Goals, by a Committee of College and University Examiners. Handbook I: Cognitive Domain.* New York: Longmans, Green.

Boeree, George. 2012. "Erik Erikson." http://webspace.ship.edu/cgboer /erikson.html.

Bronson, Po, and Ashley Merryman. 2010. "The Creativity Crisis." *Newsweek,* July 10.

Caine, Renate Numella, and Geoffrey Caine. 1991. *Affective Dimensions of Learning.* Medford, MA: North Central Regional Educational Laboratory.

———. 1997. *Education on the Edge of Possibility.* Alexandria, VA: Association for Supervision and Curriculum Development.

Clayton, Marlynn K., and Mary Beth Forton. 2001. *Classroom Spaces That Work.* Greenfield, MA: Northeast Foundation for Children.

Clemmer, Jim. 2012. "Growing the Distance: Timeless Principles for Personal, Career, and Family Success." http://www.jimclemmer.com /online-book-store-audio-leadership-books-leadership-management -time-management.php.

Collins, Francis, and Karin Jegalian. 2012. "Human Genome Project." http://ask.healthline.com/galecontent/human-genome-project.

Conklin, Wendy. 2006. *Instructional Strategies for Diverse Learners.* Huntington Beach, CA: Shell Education.

———. 2011. *Higher Order-Thinking Skills to Develop 21st Century Learners.* Huntington Beach, CA: Shell Education.

Cornell, Paul. 2002. "The Impact of Changes in Teaching and Learning on Furniture and the Learning Environment." *New Directions for Teaching & Learning* 92: 33–43.

The Creativity Centre. 2012. "What is creativity?" http://creativitycentre .weebly.com/creativity.html.

Cropley, Arthur. 2011. *Creativity in Education and Learning: A Guide for Teachers and Educators.* New York: Routledge.

Csikszentmihalyi, Mihaly. 1996. *Creativity: Flow and the Psychology of Discovery and Invention.* New York: Harper Collins.

da Vinci Inventions. 2012. "Helicopter (Aerial Screw)." http://www.da -vinci-inventions.com/aerial-screw.aspx.

Dacey, John. 1989a. *Fundamentals of Creative Thinking.* Lexington, MA: D. C. Heath/Lexington Books.

———. 1989b. "Peak Periods of Creative Growth Across the Life Span." *Journal of Creative Behavior* 23 (4): 224–247.

———. 1989c. "Discriminating Characteristics of the Families of Highly Creative Adolescents." *Journal of Creative Behavior* 23 (4): 263–271.

Dacey, John, and Lisa Fiore. 2000. *Your Anxious Child.* San Francisco, CA: Jossey-Bass.

Dacey, John, and Kathleen Lennon. 1999. *Understanding Creativity: The Interplay of Biological, Psychological and Social Factors.* San Francisco, CA: Jossey-Bass.

Dacey, John, and Alex Packer. 1992. *The Nurturing Parent.* New York: Simon & Schuster.

Dacey, John, John Travers, and Lisa Fiore. 2009. *Human Development Across the Lifespan*, seventh edition. New York: McGraw-Hill.

Dacey, John, and Lynne Weygint. 2002. *The Joyful Family.* San Francisco, CA: Conari.

de Bono, Edward. 1970. *Lateral Thinking: Creativity Step by Step.* New York: Harper and Row.

Diamond, Marian, and Janet Hopson. 1998. *Magic Trees of the Mind: How to Nurture Your Child's Intelligence, Creativity, and Healthy Emotions from Birth through Adolescence.* New York: Dutton.

Doidge, Norman. 2007. *The Brain that Changes Itself: Stories of Personal Triumph from the Frontiers of Brain Science.* New York: Penguin Books.

Dudek, Mark. 2000. *Architecture of Schools: The New Learning Environments.* Woburn, MA: Architectural Press.

Enchanted Mind. 2012. "Creativity Test" http://enchantedmind.com/html /creativity/iq_tests/creativity_test.html.

Erikson, Erik. 1963. *Childhood and Society.* New York: W. W. Norton & Company.

FairTest. 2012. "What's Wrong With Standardized Tests?" http://fairtest .org/facts/whatwron.htm.

Finkle, S., and L. Torp. 1995. *Introductory Documents.* Aurora, IL: Center for Problem-Based Learning.

Fleith, Denise de Souza. 2000. "Teacher and Student Perceptions of Creativity in the Classroom Environment." *Roeper Review* 22 (3): 148–153.

Frankl, Victor. 1985. *Man's Search for Meaning.* New York: Washington Square Press.

Gardner, Howard. 1984. *Art, Mind, and Brain: A Cognitive Approach to Creativity.* New York: Basic Books.

Gardner, Howard, and Ellen Winner. 1986. "Attitudes and Attributes: Children's Understanding of Metaphor and Sarcasm." In *Perspectives on Intellectual Development, The Minnesota Symposia on Child Psychology* 19: 131–152.

Gleick, James. 2006. *Chaos: Making a New Science.* New York: Penguin.

Gordon, William, and Tony Poze. 1980a. SES Synectics and Gifted Education Today. *Gifted Child Quarterly* 24: 147–151.

———. 1980b. *The New Art of Possible.* Cambridge, MA: Porpoise Books.

Grangaard, Ellen. 1993. "Effects of Color and Light on Selected Elementary Students." Unpublished doctoral dissertation. Las Vegas, NV: University of Nevada. (ERIC Document Reproduction Service No. ED 383445).

Grenoble, Ryan. 2012. "Sun Jifa, Chinese Man, Creates DIY Prosthetic Limbs After Losing Hands In A Fishing Accident." Accessed October 4, 2012. http://www.huffingtonpost.com/2012/08/15/sun-jifa-prosthetic -hands_n_1777168.html.

Harp, Bill. 1988. "When the Principal Asks: 'Is All That Drama Taking Valuable Time Away from Reading?'" *The Reading Teacher* 41: 938–940.

Heard, Georgia, and Jennifer McDonough. 2009. *A Place for Wonder: Reading and Writing Nonfiction in the Primary Grades.* Portland, ME: Stenhouse.

Heitlin, Liana. 2012. "National Teacher of the Year: Give Us a Career Path." http://dcschoolreform.org/news/national-teacher-year-give-us -career-path.

Helie, Sebastien, and Ron Sun. 2010. "Incubation, Insight and Creative Problem Solving: A Unified Theory and a Connectionist Model." *Psychological Review* 117 (3): 994–1024.

Heylighen, Frances, and Johan Bollen. 2012. "S*uperBRAIN*." http://earthportals.com/superbrain.html.

Hunter, Jill, and Rita Mitchell. 1997. "Genetics and Inheritance." http://www.dartmouth.edu/~cbbc/courses/bio4/bio4-1997/01-Genetics .html.

International Center for Studies in Creativity. 2012. "Optimal Learning in Optimal Contexts: The Role of Self-Determination in Education." http://buffalostate.edu/creativity/.

Investopedia. 2010. "SWOT Analysis." Accessed October 4, 2012. http://www.investopedia.com/terms/s/swot.asp.

ITS. 2012. "The Road to a Solution—Generating Ideas." http://www.tuition.com.hk/ideas.htm.

Jackson, Philip, and Samuel Messick. 1965. "The Person, the Product, and the Response: Conceptual Problems in the Assessment of Creativity." *Journal of Personality* 33 (3): 309–329.

"Jessica's 'Daily Affirmation.'" 2009. YouTube™ video, 0:50. Uploaded June 16, 2009 by dmchatster. http://www.youtube.com/ watch?v=qR3rK0kZFkg.

Komendat, Sarah. 2010. "Creative Classroom Designs." *Creative Studies Graduate Student Master's Projects* 54. Accessed October 4, 2012. http://digitalcommons.buffalostate.edu/creativeprojects/54.

Kurzweil, Ray. 2012. *How to Create a Mind: The Secret of Human Thought Revealed*. New York: Viking.

Landrum, Eric. 1990. "Maier's 1931 Two-String Problem Revisited: Evidence for Spontaneous Transfer?" *Psychological Reports* 67 (3f): 1079–1088.

Larson, Carl, and Frank LaFasto. 1989. *Teamwork: What Must Go Right/ What Can Go Wrong.* Thousand Oaks, CA: Sage Publications.

Latzke, Jeff. 2012. "Thunder Coach Scott Brooks Says Early Losses All Part of Learning to Win." *The Washington Times*, June 7.

Lebeau, Mary. 2012. "Teaching the Virtues: Courage." Accessed October 4, 2012. http://parenting.kaboose.com/behavior/emotional-social -development/teaching-virtues-courage-2.html.

Lehrer, Jonah. 2012. *Imagine: How Creativity Works.* New York: Houghton Mifflin.

Malloy, Emmett. 2010. *The White Stripes: Under Great White Northern Lights.* WEA/Reprise.

Mann, Merlin. 2008. "Attention & Ambiguity: The Non-Paradox of Creative Work." *Psychology Today: The Creative Personality*, August 20.

Mednick, Sarnoff, and Martha Mednick. 1967. *Examiner's Manual: Remote Associates Test.* Boston, MA: Houghton Mifflin.

Michalko, Michael. 2006. *Thinkertoys: A Handbook of Creative-Thinking Techniques.* Berkeley, CA: Ten Speed Press.

Millar, Garnet. 1995. *E. Paul Torrance, "The Creativity Man": An Authorized Biography.* Norwood, NJ: Ablex Publishing.

Morgane, Peter. 1970. "Raúl Hernández-Peón 1924–1968." *Physiology & Behavior* 5(4): 379–388.

National Public Radio. 2012. *Failure: The F-Word Silicon Valley Loves and Hates.* Washington, DC: National Public Radio.

Osborn, Alex. 1953. *Applied Imagination.* New York: Scribner's.

The Painter's Keys. 2012. "Leonardo da Vinci Art Quotes." http://quote
.robertgenn.com/auth_search.php?authid=243.

Paintner, Christine. 2011. *The Artist's Rule: Nurturing Your Creative Soul
with Monastic Wisdom*. New York: Ave Maria Press.

Panamericana School of Art and Design. 2012. "Creativity Test."
http://www.toxel.com/inspiration/2009/05/06/school-of-art-and
-design-creativity-test/.

Piaget, Jean. 1936. *La Naissance De L'intelligence Chez L'enfant. [Emergence of
Intelligence in the Child*. Neuchatel, Switzerland: Delachaux et Nieslé.

Piirto, Jane. 1991. "Why Are There So Few (Creative Women: Visual
Artists, Mathematicians, Scientists, Musicians)?" *Roeper Review* 13 (3):
142–147.

Prieto, Maria, Joaquin Parra, Mercedes Ferrándo, Carmen Ferrándiz,
Maria Bermejo, and Cristina Sánchez. 2006. "Creative Abilities in
Early Childhood." *Journal of Early Childhood Research* (4): 277–289.

rCAB©. 2011. "Runco Creative Assessment Battery." http://www
.creativitytestingservices.com/rCAB.html.

Rhem, James. 1998. "Problem-Based Learning: An Introduction." *The
National Teaching & Learning Forum* 9 (1).

Rogak, Lisa. 2009. *Haunted Heart: The Life and Times of Stephen King*. New
York: St. Martin's Press/Thomas Dunne Books.

Sarkisian, Ellen. 2012. "Working in Groups." http://isites.harvard.edu/fs
/html/icb.topic58474/wigintro.html.

Sawyer, Keith. 2003. *Improvised Dialogues: Emergence and Creativity in
Conversation*. New York: Ablex Publishing.

Schoenherr, Neil. 2006. "You too can be creative; it just takes hard work." Accessed October 4, 2012. http://news.wustl.edu/news/Pages/6451 .aspx.

Shapiro, Deane H., Shauna L. Shapiro, John A. Astin, and Johanna Shapiro. 2010. "Self Control." In The *Corsini Encyclopedia of Psychology* 1–2. http://onlinelibrary.wiley.com/doi/10.1002/9780470479216 .corpsy0833/abstract.

Shneiderman, Ben. 2007. "Creativity Support Tools." http://cacm.acm .org/magazines/2007/12/5511-creativity-support-tools-accelerating -discovery-and-innovation/fulltext.

Siegelman, Ellen. 1990. *Metaphor and Meaning in Psychotherapy.* New York: The Guilford Press.

Slade, Neil. 2012. "The Frontal Lobes Supercharge." http://www.neilslade .com/art/Brain/chap1.html.

Sternberg, Robert, and Todd Lubart. 1995. *Defying the Crowd: Cultivating Creativity in a Culture of Conformity.* New York: Free Press.

STS. 2012. "Torrance Test of Creative Thinking." http://ststesting .com/2005giftttct.html.

TED. 2012. "The TED Book." http://thetedbook.com/home/.

Torrance, Ellis Paul. 1961. "Factors Affecting Creative Thinking in Children: An Interim Research Report." *Merrill-Palmer Quarterly* 7: 171–180.

———. 1995. *Why Fly: A Philosophy of Creativity.* New York: Ablex Publishing Corporation.

Treffinger, Donald, Scott Isaken, and K. Brian Stead-Dorval. 2006. *Creative Problem Solving: An Introduction.* Waco, TX: Prufrock Press.

Tucker-Ladd, Clayton. 2004. "Psychological Self-Help." Chapter 14. http://www.psychologicalselfhelp.org/.

Wallas, Graham. 1926. *The Art of Thought*. New York: Harcourt.

Welsh, George. 2012. "The Welsh Figure Preference Test." http://www.mindgarden.com/products/wfpts.htm.

WETA. 2012. "Reading Rockets." Accessed October 2, 2012. http://www.readingrockets.org/strategies/visual_imagery.

Whitkin, Josh. 2012. "Flow in Real-Time Physical Prototyping of Video Games." http://whitkin.com/?p=62.

Williams, Frank E. 1970. *Classroom Ideas for Encouraging Thinking and Feeling*. Buffalo, NY: D.O.K. Publishers.

———. 1982. *Classroom Ideas for Encouraging Thinking and Feeling*. Volume 2. Buffalo, NY: D.O.K. Publishers.

# Literature Cited

## Books

Andersen, Hans Christian. (1836) 1982. *The Little Mermaid*. New York: Random House Books for Young Readers.

Barrett, Judi. 1978. *Cloudy With a Chance of Meatballs*. New York: Atheneum Books for Young Readers.

Collins, Suzanne. 2010. *The Hunger Games*. New York: Scholastic Press.

Cosmo, A. J. 2012. *The Monster That Ate My Socks*. New York: Thought Bubble.

Curtis, Christopher Paul. 1999. *Bud, Not Buddy*. New York: Yearling.

Dahl, Roald. 1964. *Charlie and the Chocolate Factory*. New York: Alfred A. Knopf.

DiCamillo, Kate. 2003. *The Tale of Despereaux*. Cambridge, MA: Candlewick Press.

Hawthorne, Nathaniel. (1850) 1994. *The Scarlet Letter*. Mineola, NY: Dover Publications.

Kinney, Jeff. 2007. *Diary of a Wimpy Kid*. New York: Amulet Books.

Lobel, Arnold. 1970. *Frog and Toad Are Friends*. New York: HarperCollins.

Macaulay, David. 1979. *Motel of the Mysteries*. New York: Houghton Mifflin.

Perrault, Charles. (1697) 1999. *Cinderella*. New York: North-South Books.

Pinkwater, Daniel Manus. 1977. *The Big Orange Splot*. New York: Scholastic.

Dr. Seuss. 1957. *The Cat In the Hat*. New York: Random House.

———. 1971. *The Lorax*. New York: Random House.

Shakespeare, William. (1599) 1986. *Romeo and Juliet*. New York: Signet Classics.

———. (1606) 1993. *Macbeth*. Mineola, NY: Dover Publications.

## Periodicals

*Journal of Creative Behavior*
    http://www.creativeeducationfoundation.org/node/60

*O: The Oprah Magazine*
    http://www.oprah.com/omagazine.html

## Visual Media

*Bolschewismus bringt Krieg, Arbeitslosigkeit und Hungersnot*
    http://www.loc.gov/pictures/item/2004665871/

*Extreme Home Makeover: Home Edition*
    http://abc.go.com/shows/extreme-makeover-home-edition

*Molly Pitcher [i.e. Molly McCauley loading cannon at Battle of Monmouth, 1778]*
    http://www.loc.gov/pictures/item/2004672798/

Salvador Dalí's *Crucifixion*
    http://www.metmuseum.org/collections/search-the-collections/210009107

*Titanic*. Directed by James Cameron. 1997. Beverly Hills, CA: Twentieth Century Fox Film Corporation.

# Visualization Teacher Resource

## Trip to the Sun Script

Today, we are going to travel into space, looking down first on our school and then speeding above Earth past the moon, past two planets, and to the sun. In order to take this trip, you have to try your best to keep your eyes closed and really listen as I'm speaking. First, let's put on our space suits, which will protect us from the extremely hot and extremely cold temperatures of outer space. These suits are also equipped with jet rockets that allow us to travel at super speeds.

Picture yourself getting into a bulky suit that is made out of very strong plastic. It probably feels pretty heavy. Visualize the color and shape of the suit. Feel the helmet that is on your head. Is it heavy? Attached to the helmet is your oxygen tank. Remember, there is no oxygen after we leave Earth's atmosphere, so don't forget to hook it up. In fact, do it now. Take the time now to check it out and see if the tank is working. We want you to be able to breathe in space. Be careful as you hook the oxygen tank to the helmet.

Now that you are properly protected from the heat and the cold, we are ready to blast off. The best feature of our special space suits is that the jet rockets are easy to control. Get ready to press the button on the glove of your left hand so that you can soar through Earth's atmosphere. Ten, nine, eight, seven, six, five, four, three, two, one—blast off! Imagine yourself flying up into the atmosphere. You are high above our school. Now slow yourself down so that you can look down and see a bird's eye view of our school. Do you see the playground in your mind? Can you see your house? Your neighborhood? The town center?

Let's power up a little higher. We are still in Earth's atmosphere. It protects us from meteors, most of which burn up before they can do any harm. As we are speeding through space, remember to watch out for meteors.

Look back at Earth. Are you high enough to see the ocean? Can you see any important geographical features you recognize? Do you see Canada? As we go higher, can you see the shape of the United States? Keep going higher. Imagine looking down at Earth from about 5,000 miles in space. You will see Earth looks like a beautiful blue and green marble. Can you make out the shape of Florida? Earth completes one rotation on its axis each day. A spot on the equator rotates at approximately 1,000 miles per hour. It is a wonder we don't get dizzy.

Look at Earth. What do you see? Oceans? Islands?

See the clouds hanging above the cold Atlantic coast off southwestern Africa? The moisture from the ocean water is causing clouds to form and will cause storms when the cold causes the vapor to turn into water. If it gets cold enough, the water will turn into sleet, ice pellets, and golf ball-sized hail.

Notice the sandy-colored Sahara Desert on the continent of Africa. Let's circle Earth and see if we can see the Great Wall of China... oh, wait. Isn't it dark in China now? Ah, yes...no Great Wall, but we can see the light of the cities.

Now that we have taken a look at Earth, let's adjust our rockets to travel 240,000 miles to the moon, our only natural satellite. First, we will explore what is called the near side of the moon. The near side of the moon is the side that always faces toward Earth while the far side always faces away.

Both the near side and the far side of the moon have a day and a night. Both receive sunlight at certain points in the moon's orbit around Earth. We just can't see the far side of the moon from Earth even when the sun is shining on it because the far side always faces away from us. Since only a few astronauts have ever seen the far side of the moon, let's check it out.

Wow! It looks as if bombs have been dropped on this side of the moon. Do you see all the craters and holes? This side looks really beaten up—many meteorites have pounded this side of the moon. There are dark spots in the middle of the craters. It looks like there have been many, many objects from outer space that have hit this side of the moon.

The near side of the moon is many shades of white and gray. Do you see the volcanic craters? Large craters formed from volcanoes scattered on the surface. Some of these craters are filled with black lava.

Let's look and see if we can see the footprints of the astronauts who landed on the moon in July 20, 1969. Oh, I see them, do you? It looks like the moon is covered in thick dust. Moondust? The footprints are exactly as they were because the moon has no atmosphere. No rain, no clouds, no wind, nothing to disturb the footprints made over 40 years ago!

Okay, I think we have to move on if we want to return to school before lunchtime. But we can't turn back until we see the star nearest Earth, our sun. Put those rockets in high gear—we are going to take a quick fly-by of the planets Venus and Mercury, too.

Since we will now be traveling about 93 million miles to the sun, we will only glance at the two planets as we fly by. We'll check out Venus on the way to the sun and Mercury on the way back.

Okay, nice job speeding up. Exciting to go so fast, isn't it? I hope your space suit is holding up. Now, slow down so we can glance at Venus on your right. It looks about the same size as Earth. Venus has an atmosphere, but we won't be visiting Venus today. Can you see the yellow clouds swirling around over there? The wind is blowing at about 250 miles per hour. On Earth, we worry when the wind blows 50 miles per hour. The clouds on Venus trap the sun's rays and make it as hot as Mercury, the planet nearest the sun.

Speaking of the sun, get those rockets ready to go faster so they can take us there. Put on a little extra sunscreen as we travel. Did you remember to put on your sunglasses? That's quite a sun glare we are experiencing.

Do you see the huge ball of exploding gas in front of you? That's really the sun! Look carefully, and you might see a solar flare shooting out the sides. We don't want to get caught in one of those, so we have to stay far away from the sun because some of those flares can travel about 200,000 miles into space. It is really hot, even in our space suits.

Can you guess how many planets the size of Earth would fit into the sun? If you guessed a million, you are correct—a million Earths would fit inside the sun! Get out your binoculars and look for the bubbling hot gases on the surface of the sun.

I see a few dark blotches on the sun. Those blotches are called "sun spots." They are really pretty big. The sun is cooler in those spots. Well, we could stay here near the sun a lot longer, but it is pretty hot. So let's turn around and go back to school.

Glance over at Mercury on our right. It is the smallest planet in our solar system. It is hard to see because of the sun's glare, but look hard. Mercury rotates on its axis much more slowly than Earth does. In the time it takes Mercury to make one rotation, Earth experiences 59 days and nights! On Mercury, the days are terribly hot and the nights are horribly cold.

Okay, prepare yourself to speed up so we can cover the long distance back to Earth and our school. Next time, we'll venture in our space suits on a path away from the sun out to the end of our solar system!

## Teacher Reflection

I wanted to assess the reactions of the students during our trip to the sun, so I asked them what they enjoyed most about this activity. Here is what they said they liked the most:

"I really liked the feeling of speed I got from traveling through space so fast!"

"It was easy to see the sun because of the way you described it."

"I thought it was easy to see almost everything you said."

"It was really cool that we could see our school from the air."

Here is what they said they liked the least:

"I just couldn't think what it must feel like to be traveling that fast. I didn't like trying to get the feeling of it."

"I was afraid we might go too close to the sun."

"The hardest thing to imagine was the Great Wall of China because you didn't really describe it."

"The hardest thing was seeing the dark side of the moon that nobody's ever seen before because I don't know what that would look like."

I wasn't surprised by this feedback. It just shows how different the students are from one another and how they have different preferences. For example, a number of the students loved the idea of speed while others liked it least. When you present a script like this, you want all students to have the same experience, but they don't. They have different levels of understanding, but for the moment, everybody can follow along—they can integrate their learning with something they know. Then, I vary the depth of the questions I ask when I follow up: some are simple and some are more complex. I also met individual needs, offering choices by asking how they would like to further investigate this topic.

This was a rather long script for them to listen to, but it's later in the year and my students have developed their ability to listen this long. It took about 20 minutes, but you could scaffold this experience by just doing three minutes of the script one day, five minutes the next day, and then finishing on the third day. That way, each succeeding day can build on what they learned the previous day.

*Notes*

*Notes*